Still
Standing

Verna Davis LaCour

BeNeveu Words, Inc.
Publishing Company
Rosenberg, Texas

Still Standing

Verna Davis LaCour

BeNeveu Words, Inc.

Publishing Company
BeNeveu Words, Inc. Publishing Company
Rosenberg, TX 77471

ISBN-13 DIGIT: 978-0-692-75906-6
ISBN-10 DIGIT: 0-692-75906-9
Library of Congress Control Number 2016951071
Manufactured in the United States of America

First Edition

Acknowledgments

I give all praise and honor to God the Father for blessing me to share my life story. I thank Him for keeping me in the palm of his hand, even when I didn't realize I was being kept. I thank Him for being my light when the path in front of me seemed dark. I thank God that John 8:36 is a part of my daily prayer of thanksgiving, Therefore, whom the Son sets free; is free indeed.

I would like to acknowledge my children, Lolita, Myranda, Beulah, Donald, Albert, and Herman for always trusting and believing in me. Before you learned about God, you had an unwavering faith that mama would take care of you and protect you. I thank you today because you've never forgotten the sacrifices made for you, therefore you make it a point to make sure I have all that I need. I've had doubts about a lot of things in my life, but there was never a doubt in how much you love me and the sacrifices you wouldn't now make for me.

Verna Davis LaCour

I would like to acknowledge my grandchildren for being the kind and loving young men and women you are. I don't have to worry because I know you are and will always be there for me. Every phone call and financial support you have given is greatly appreciated. You have always been a source of laughter and fun. I see your parents in each of you and that is rewarding within itself. Spoiling you has been easy and my pleasure. And yes, I will continue to do so as long as God gives me breath and the ability.

I would like to acknowledge my great grandchildren. You are the fourth generation of God's blessings to me. I find myself asking God, "What did I do to deserve a family as great and as large as the one you have given me?" Your ages range from 20 years old down to newborn. I love you all the same and I pray for you every day. To the older great grandchildren, I am very proud of you. You must understand, every sibling and cousin will look at, reach for, and try to surpass the goals you set as the head of your generation. Never take that lightly, aim high and be better than ever before. Live your life as if God is watching, because he is. I love you!

I would like to acknowledge all of my family and friends. You have been there for not only me but my children. You are a part of the village that has made my life as special as it is. To those who have married into the family, all I have is thank you. Curtis and Thomas you have made my daughters very happy. Seeing you live marriage the way God intended gives me great joy. To all of my family and friends, thank you for your love, your support, your encouragement, and mostly your prayers. I love you and I appreciate you.

I would like to acknowledge Ernest Lambert of Lambert Photography and Graphics and Keith T. Walker for my beautiful book cover. I would like to thank Janae Hampton for editing my first novel and Jennifer Lee for her helpful insight while critiquing my work.

Last, but certainly not least, I would like to acknowledge and thank Terry Telsee for giving me the inspiration to share my story. It took a few years to get started, but you kept encouraging me to be a source of help to others. With each conversation we shared you helped me to see, it was only by God's grace that I am "Still Standing."

Introduction

Today is such a beautiful day. I'm sitting on the porch in my white rocking chair drinking a cup of coffee and enjoying a morning of perfect weather, that doesn't happen much in Houston. It's either to hot and humid or just too humid period to enjoy being outside. I've been thinking about how so many people ask me, "How do I keep looking so young and have such a positive attitude when things around me are going crazy?" They don't understand it when I say, "I've been through much worse than this." They really seem puzzled when I say it with a smile on my face. After a conversation with a couple of friends a few days ago I started thinking about all the things I've been through and how I'm still standing and in as good a shape as I'm in. I want to share my story to give someone hope and the courage to hang on and push forward.

Chapter 1

Well, I guess I'll start at the beginning. I was born in the small town of DeQuincy, Louisiana. I was the fourth of six children, including two older brothers I didn't meet until we were adults. My parents were BeMentria and Mianda Davis. My mother moved to Freeport, Texas when I was very young. (But later went to live with her). My sister Beulah and I lived with our dad in Louisiana. My father was tall, about six feet and a few inches tall. I remember he had coal black wavy hair, and high cheek bones. I would describe his skin as the color of dark chocolate candy. Everyone says he was very handsome, and Beulah and I got our beautiful looks and coal black hair from him.

We lived with my aunt, my daddy's sister Thelma Sudds. One of the fond memories I have of living there is the well in the back yard where we drew our water. My dad would always tell me, "Mama, stay away from the well." He was always afraid I would fall in because I was curious about everything. Beulah and I were spoiled by our dad and aunt. My sister and I were very happy and carefree. We were always together and I would say, she was my best friend. She was quiet most of the time. It seemed she was always thinking about something. I admired her because she was very smart. She watched over me and showered me with love. At first I thought it was to make up for our mom not being there, but I realized, she loved me so deeply simply because I was her sister.

Soon my dad and aunt began to notice Beulah would tire out very easily. At first they thought it was because she seemed fragile (that's the term they used when describing her). After a few doctor visits, they confirmed that she had heart disease. They became more protective over her after her diagnosis. I was okay because she always assured me that she was okay and not to worry.

My dad and aunt worried about us when they went to work. They were brakemen for the railroad. Beulah and I knew what time the train would come by and, because we didn't live far from the tracks we would stand there and wave at them. They always had something for us and would throw it to us as they passed by. It was also their way of checking to make sure we were doing fine.

My first memory of pain was the death of my father. Daddy passed away when I was around five years old. Back then, when people died they held wake services at the house. I didn't really understand what was going on. After all of our family and friends left I waited for daddy to come tuck me in, and tell me goodnight, like he did every evening. After he didn't come to me I did the next best thing, I went where he was. I saw him in the casket and thought he was asleep. I went into the kitchen, got the stool, and pulled it up to the casket. I got my blanket and climbed in with him. My aunt and sister were calling for me but I wouldn't answer, I wanted to stay with my dad. By the time they found me I was asleep, resting in my dad's arms. I didn't know that would be the last time I would sleep in his arms or be able to see or touch him. It was never the same after that. Beulah and I missed our dad very much.

Aunt Thelma watched over Beulah real closely, she was afraid the death of our father would be too much for her heart to handle. In the midst of her weakness she became strong. I was afraid now that she would go away where daddy went. Beulah being the kind and loving sister she always was, made sure to remind me, daily, that she was okay and she wasn't going to leave me. Beulah and I stayed in DeQuincy for two years after dad was laid to rest.

Chapter 2

Beulah and I moved to Bay City, TX to live with our mom and some of her relatives. For a few years we would travel back to DeQuincy to spend summers with Aunt Thelma. While we were there, our aunt would allow us to go to the movies. We could only go up the stairway and enter through the back door and sit to the back of the movie theater. That's the only place we were allowed to sit back then. I noticed we couldn't go downstairs to purchase popcorn like the other movie goers. Beulah simply told me, "We'll eat our popcorn when we get home." I had no idea she was protecting me from the pain of prejudice.

When Beulah and I arrived in Bay City we saw mama had given birth to a set of twins, a boy named Charlie and a girl named Clara. They were two years old at the time. No one explained to me why my mama had babies when my dad had passed away a few years ago. Back then, you couldn't ask questions about, what they considered grown folk's business. I realized I could enjoy being the older sister now. After five years I was no longer the baby of the family. I was happy that we were all together. That feeling only lasted a few years. Our mom died by the time I was nine years old. I remember being sad, but I didn't feel the pain as deeply as I had when my dad passed away.

After mama was laid to rest we went to live with her sister in Freeport, TX. There was always a lot of children living there. Well, I guess that should've been expected, with my parents' four children and my auntie's five. One of the craziest memories I have of living with my aunt and all of my cousins was bath time. We had what was called the First Water. That's where the girls would bathe first and then the tub had to be emptied, cleaned, and refilled for the boys. We usually had to change the bath water several times before everyone was clean for the night. There were four of us in the bed I slept in. Our bed was right next to the window. Because there was no central air we slept with the windows up and most of the time with no screens on them. Directly outside of the window was a big peach tree. That was where the big wood rats would hang around so they could eat whatever peaches fell from the tree. I remember sometimes we would see foot prints where the rats had crossed over the bed as we slept, but they never bit any of us. I guess they were too full from the peaches. Those rats acted like they were part of the family, and liked playing hide and seek with us, because we never saw them during the day.

There were two sets of twins living in the house. One set was identical twin boys, the other set was my sister and brother. My cousins were called Big Jay and Lil Jay. Another fond memory was, when Big Jay would get into trouble he would change his name to George. Auntie would say, "Well George, you're going to get a whipping today." We would all laugh because Big Jay never figured out that George was still getting a whipping no matter how many times he used that name.

Because we had no school bus to pick us up, we walked to school each day. It didn't seem like a long way for us because there was always a group of us, laughing and playing around, so we had fun most of the time. But, there was my neighbor Eugene, for some reason we always got into fights on our way home. I guess they weren't real fights because we always hugged and said, "I'll see you later," by the time we made it to the house. We all walked home for lunch every day except Fridays. We ate at school on that day because they served sandwiches and ginger bread. That was special for us.

I was the odd kid that loved going to school and hated when I had to miss. We were only allowed to miss school when we had to pick cotton. If we wanted

Still Standing

extra clothes or supplies for school, we had to pick pecans also. Close to the end of the school year, thru the first few months of school, I spent a lot of my time in the cotton field or on the pecan grove working for the things I needed for school.

Chapter 3

As I sit here thinking back, I don't know why, but I lived in a lot of different places when I was young. I remember staying with my cousins Calvin and Evelyn. We lived on the main road which is now called Almeda Rd. My Aunt Rae worked in Freeport and each day the bus driver would stop so my aunt could give me whatever gift she had bought for me.

I was later sent to live in Bay City on a farm with more relatives, my great aunt Ma Magg and Papa Henry. I remember Ma Magg being mean. She was mean for no other reason than to be mean. Papa Henry was just the opposite. He had a kind and loving heart. I remember Ma Magg making me feed the hogs while I was there. I never understood why I was sent away to live with someone else when I came home from school one day. As mean as Ma Magg was, I thought everyone was okay with me living there.

From there, I was sent to Angleton, TX to live

Still Standing

with Uncle Willie and Aunt Rae. Uncle Willie spoiled me and would never allow my auntie to whip me while he was home. Because I wasn't disciplined when Aunt Rae whipped everyone else my whippings piled up. Each time my aunt thought I was supposed to be disciplined she would stack a switch in the corner for me. When Uncle Willie would leave, and go to town to run errands my aunt whipped me with every switch that was stacked in that corner. I even got whippings for things I didn't do. I had to go to school in the middle of summer with sweaters on to hide the welts on my arms, and long socks to hide the scars on my legs. As sweet as she was when I stayed with my cousins, I didn't understand why she whipped me so much when I came to live with them.

My cousins came to live with us at Uncle Willie's and Aunt Rae's. With so many children in the house we all were given chores. One of my favorite chores was having to help sweep the front yard. With no grass anywhere, we swept the dirt. We didn't know you could make dirt look so pretty, but we did. We didn't have much, with so many kids having to be taken care of, so we made our own toys. The girls would make dolls with soda bottles, and grass rope, used by the ice man to carry blocks of ice, for doll hair. We made a little kitchen from crate boxes. We made beautiful mud cakes and picked china berries from the tree in the front yard for our peas. We had lots of fun when we were all together. Even with all the whippings I received I felt having my sisters and brother with me was worth it.

I started working at the age of twelve years old. I got my first job ironing khaki uniforms for the people my aunt worked for. Aunt Rae was also the cook at the local hospital. There were only 16 beds in the entire hospital, so there wasn't a lot of patients to care for. Beulah and I went to work with Aunt Rae to help cook the evening meals. A lot of times Beulah and I would prepare all the meals. "Let me show you how it's done," she always teased. I watched her closely, hoping one day to be able to cook just like her.

"You'll get it lil sis," she'd tell me with the beautiful smile she always had for me. I did my best to never let her down. By the time I was 13 years old I could prepare the meals, and serve them by myself if necessary.

One day at work Beulah was making cheese sandwiches. She didn't realize the burner hadn't come on when she looked down to see how high the flames were. By the time she bent over, the flames burst into her face. Although we were at the hospital and they treated her right away, I was so afraid. She swallowed some of the flames and her eyebrows and eyelashes were burnt, she was blessed not to be injured more seriously. She spent the night at the hospital and went home the next day. Thank God it was one of those days we only had five patients admitted. I finished the evening meals and cleaned the kitchen as quickly as possible so I could go check on my sister, and spend time with her before it was time for me to go home. Because Beulah knew me so well, she knew I was scared without me saying a word. She held my hand and told me, "Stop worrying, I'm going to be fine."

"I don't want you to stay here by yourself. Maybe I can stay with you," I whispered so no one could hear me but her.

"I need you to be a big girl and watch Charlie and Clara until I get home tomorrow," she answered back softly. I nodded my head and hugged her again. The doctor and Aunt Rae stopped at her bed to tell me it was time to go so she could rest. I didn't want to leave my sister, but I knew I had to go. Once I got home I didn't talk much that night. No one seemed to understand how worried I was about Beulah. We had been together all of our lives. I was still somewhat afraid she would leave me like our parents did, and never come back.

As we got older I wanted to go places, but couldn't go unless Beulah was going with me. By the time I was 14 years old I noticed Beulah was sick a lot and weak most of the time. When she felt well she would go with me so I wouldn't miss out on having fun with my friends. We went to our regular Friday night Record Hop dance. It didn't matter how much fun I was having I always made time to go check on Beulah, as she sat in the corner, watching me. I was a great dancer. Beulah always told me how much she liked to see me dance. I won a few dancing contests and made sure Beulah was the first to see whatever prize I won. Even today I get teary eyed at the sacrifices she made for me just so I could enjoy being a teenager. I was allowed to play in the band at school. My instrument of choice was the French horn. I got a chance to travel with the band without Beulah being present. She always hugged me and told me, "Have fun! I'll be waiting for you, so you can tell me about the game and your performance."

While attending Marshall High, Mrs. Lottie was my homemaking teacher. She was like a mother to me. She taught me about my body and the changes it would go through as I got older. She couldn't tell me when these changes would come, but to always be prepared. Well, I found out while playing volleyball in gym class. I had on a pretty white skirt with bright red apples on it. It was a long flowing skirt with a few heavily starched cancan slips under it. I was running around and suddenly my slips weren't feeling right. I ran to Mrs. Lottie and she knew what was going on. I was scared because I didn't know what was happening. She helped me get clean and explained everything she

Still Standing

had taught me before. I remember her wiping my tears, comforting me and reassuring me it was all a part of growing up.

We went to Spiritual Temple Church each Sunday. It was there I began to remember what my Aunt Thelma and Daddy taught me about having faith in God. I began to hold on to that faith when Uncle Willie passed away. Aunt Rae was sad a lot, but I guess she didn't have time to grieve because she had to take care of all of us. Somehow, Aunt Rae was able to buy a black and white television. We were so happy. We were so grateful we didn't care that it wasn't a color tv. Soon after, we got a telephone installed. We had what was called a Party Line. You could hear other people's conversations. We weren't supposed to listen, but we took turns listening anyway and we had fun doing it, until Aunt Rae would catch us. Again life was good. We missed Uncle Willie, but Aunt Rae kept everything together.

Chapter 4

Aunt Rae passed when I was 15 years old. The night she died I had to be rushed to the hospital because a bug flew into my ear. The bug's humming in my eardrum was very painful. By the time the doctor came in to check my ear the bug had flown out. Everyone kept saying it was my way of dealing with Auntie's death. After Aunt Rae was laid to rest our cousins went back to live with their mother. We were on our own again. It was Beulah, me, and our twin sister and brother. Beulah did all she could to take care of us by herself. Finally, Beulah and the twins moved to Houston while I remained in Angleton. I wanted to finish school at Marshall High with all my friends. Beulah left me in the care of a family friend, Nanny. Although she was nice and treated me like her daughter, I started missing my sisters and brother.

Beulah brought me to Houston to live with her and the twins. We lived on Hutchins Street in an apartment located in back of what was called the Pink

Still Standing

House. She enrolled me in Jack Yates High School. Back then the school was located in what is now Ryan's Middle School. Coming from the country I didn't know schools were so large. I stood in front of the school in awe. I wasn't used to school buildings with so many windows, rooms, and stairs. As nervous as I was, I was still excited to be going to a big city school. Knowing how overwhelmed I was, Beulah asked one of her friends from church named Thelma to show me around the school. I thought I had it memorized until after my first class and it was time to go to lunch, and then on to more classes.

After one week of getting lost, being late, and completely confused on such a large campus I asked Beulah if I could return to Angleton, where everything was on the same level. As I sit here and think about that five day adventure, there's nothing I can say I remember about Jack Yates except how big it was. Even today I laugh and say, "Oh well, I tried."

Chapter 5

I was glad to be back home, ole Marshall High. I was happy to be back amongst my friends, the people I knew. Unbeknownst to me one of the toughest guys on campus had taken a liking to me. I didn't have a boyfriend, but I knew of one boy named Johnnie that liked me and I liked him also. When Herman found out Johnnie liked me, he told him to stay away from me because I was his girlfriend. Because everyone was afraid of Herman, Johnnie wouldn't look at me, let alone speak, neither would any of the other guys on campus. I was afraid of Herman too but somehow I still ended up with him

While I was in Angleton, Beulah fell in love with Bobby Turner. When they were married I was so happy for her. I remember how beautiful she looked in her wedding gown. Her smile was so bright it seemed to light up the room. I knew she loved Bobby and he loved her so much. I sat there wondering if someday I would have a husband like Bobby that would make me smile like my sister. I knew she was in good hands and I didn't have to worry about her being alone with Charlie and Clara. They were 12 years old and quite a handful.

I went back to Angleton while the twins stayed in Houston with Bobby and Beulah. Soon after returning I got pregnant by Herman. I was afraid so I went back to Houston and stayed with my sister and her husband. I got very sick and had to go into the hospital. I was admitted to Jefferson Davis hospital for four months. For some strange reason the doctors thought I had tuberculosis. They put me on a quarantined floor for those with highly contagious diseases. While there, I saw two people die before my eyes. Because I was pregnant they moved me to an area with less people, but they were still all very sick. While still in isolation, on June 22, 1959, I gave birth to my first son, Herman Hall Jr. At 8lbs, 3oz, he was a healthy bundle of joy. I thanked God that he had not been affected by being on that floor. Herman's sister Pheobe and his mother, Erma came to Houston to pick Herman Jr. up from the hospital. They took him to Angleton where they took care of him while I remained in the hospital to be treated.

While I was in the hospital, Beulah became very sick and weak. On July 4, 1959 my life changed forever, when Alexander, our longtime family friend, walked through the door I knew from the look on his face something was wrong. I never thought it would be, Beulah had passed away. My first response was disbelief. Then I felt a sense of loss and pain that I haven't felt since that day. I was allowed to go home so I could attend the funeral. I stood at her casket thinking, about how beautiful she looked. I sat through the service on the front row with Bobby and my siblings. I couldn't stop crying. I looked at her son, Bobby Jr. He had her beautiful smile already. Bobby Sr. was holding on to him very tightly. Somehow, I thought, he could feel Beulah's warmth through their son. Tears continued to fall as my big sister and best friend lay there before me. Beulah had always been there for me, now she was gone like daddy, my mom, and my aunt. She was who I talked to and who I leaned on. Even as sick as she was, I never thought she would die. I felt lost, I felt alone. After she was laid to rest I had to go back to the hospital and the twins went back to live with Bobby. I knew he loved them and would continue to take care of them.

After another two months in the hospital the doctors realized I didn't have tuberculous and sent me home. I went back to Angleton, got my son, and we went to live with Nanny.

Just sitting here thinking about Beulah is painful, yet refreshing. I can hear her saying, "I'm ok. You go and have some fun." I love her with an

Still Standing

everlasting love. My love for her will never be spoken in past tense. It is as real today as it was all those years ago. I have to take a break now. Thinking back, being filled with so many different emotions is draining.

Chapter 6

By the time I was 17 years old I had already endured so much. Never in my wildest imagination could I have guessed the worst was still yet to come. I came back to Houston with Herman and our son. We moved into the apartment behind the Pink House. With no one to talk to or to guide me I was soon pregnant with my second child. When Herman realized I was pregnant again he decided we should get married. I wasn't asked, therefore I didn't have a choice. Never could I have imagined how mean, evil, and jealous Herman was or would become.

There were times I thought he couldn't start his day off without hitting me. He didn't need a reason nor did he make up one. I didn't think life nor marriage was supposed to be like this. Herman would beat me whenever he felt the need to do so. The first time he punched me with his fist I saw stars and nearly passed out. As I lay on the floor he hit me several more times then told me to get up, go wash my face, and cook him something to eat. I couldn't believe what I was hearing, but was too afraid to question it. I did everything I was told, but the beatings kept coming. Everyone knew it was happening, but no one talked about it nor did they try to help me. When Herman would leave Alex (short for Alexander) would take me into the Pink House and ice down my bruises. He made sure I was home before Herman returned. He treated me with kindness, like a daughter. He hated the way Herman treated me, but was too old to do anything about it.

On June 26· 1960, God blessed me with a beautiful little girl. One look at her angelic face and her name came to me right away. "Lolita, that's your name lil angel," I smiled down at her. By the time we went home from the hospital she was already spoiled. I loved holding her hands. I couldn't believe how soft her face was. I didn't get a chance to bond with Herman Jr. because I stayed in the hospital the first few months of his life. Holding my baby girl became my safe place in the crazy messed up life I was living.

One evening Herman walked into the house. I was sitting on the sofa when he came over and hit me so hard Lolita flew out of my arms onto the sofa. "Who is he?" Herman shouted. I had no idea who he was talking about. "Answer me!" he yelled. I was afraid to look up at him, but I had to or I would get hit again.

"What are you talking about?" I asked softly.

"That nigga at the church!"

"There's no one at the church. I don't know what you're talking about." I knew that wasn't what he wanted to hear. He proved it by kicking me in my side.

"You're a damn liar!" I was too afraid to say anything else. He was in one of his jealous rages, so trying to explain would only make it worse. "You lying bitch! No one goes to church just to be going!" Herman picked me up and choked me. I kept fighting to get his hands loose. He dropped me back on the floor. Lolita was screaming so I tried to reach over to comfort her. That was a big mistake. He grabbed me and punched me several more times with his fist. He picked me up, slapped me across the face then threw me on the sofa. "Shut that damn baby up!" He yelled.

I put Lolita in my arms and held her tightly. I sat there rocking her trying to calm her down. I picked up her bottle from the floor. "Shhh, you have to stop crying," I kept whispering to her. I sang a verse of Precious Lord and she finally stopped crying to finish her bottle. "My beautiful baby girl, I pray you never know such evil." She looked at me with such tenderness, as if she understood me. She smiled as tears flowed down my face.

Still Standing

◊ ◊ ◊ ◊ ◊

Within a few months of Lolita being born I was pregnant with my third child. Herman wasn't as abusive when I was pregnant. So being pregnant again wasn't the worst thing in the world. For some reason I wanted to have a baby shower with this baby. I had one girl and one boy already so this little bundle would give me a second boy or girl. It was kinda exciting wanting to know the sex. Herman forbid having the shower, but it didn't take the happiness and joy I felt away. Most of the time I had to hide my excitement about the baby. Herman associated me being happy or excited about anything as disrespectful to him or that I was hiding something from him. When Lolita was quiet or sleeping I would sit and rub my stomach as the baby kicked and moved. Herman would sit and watch me. He caught me by surprise one evening. He walked over and slapped me. "Put your shirt down! Why are you always rubbing on your damn stomach?" he asked sharply.

"I like feeling the baby move," I answered softly. I didn't want him to think I was being smart mouthed.

"It's not like it's your first baby," he said still standing over me with his hand now balled into a fist.

"I know, but this one kicks harder than Jr. or

Lolita did," I answered with my head down.

He looked at me like I was crazy, but he didn't hit me again. "Just keep your shirt down when I'm around. I don't want to see that shit!" He made the statement while walking off. I didn't get hit that evening or for the next two months. On August 31st I gave birth to a beautiful baby girl. From the moment I saw her I knew I would name her after my mother. "Your name is Myranda, a beautiful name for a beautiful baby girl," I said as I kept kissing her on the forehead. "We have to pray your daddy think its okay." I asked Herman if it was okay. Once he knew it was my mom's name, my baby got to keep her name.

By the time Myranda was two months old the abuse started back. If I went to the store and the line was to long, I got beat because he assumed I was meeting someone. Heck, I just needed groceries and Pet Milk so he and the kids could eat. I got jumped on if I stayed at the laundromat to long. It wasn't like I could control the heat on the dryers, especially for the cheap towels he insisted on bringing home for us to use. The beatings were worse when his anger stemmed from jealousy. Those beatings were more than I could bare. They left me bruised and sore for days after the assault. After being beaten so long for a lie, I decided to make the lie truth. I was getting beat for it anyway. With his capacity for cheating I didn't understand why he would care if I had someone else on the side or not.

I remember sitting on the sofa one evening playing with Lolita and Myranda while Herman Jr (his nickname by now was Bomb) was playing on the floor. Herman walked through the door. He wasn't alone. A guy walked in behind him and stopped in the doorway. He looked to be about 6' 5" and weighed about 300 lbs. His hair was cut short and his eyes looked like they were borrowed from the devil. Herman called him into the bedroom. Earl, was his name and it was one I would soon come to hate.

They stayed in the room for a few minutes, came out and left out the front door. Herman went first. Earl stopped at the top step and turned back to look at me. He didn't smile nor frown he just stared at me. When he closed the door I realized he had scared me so bad I was shaking. I sensed evil from him like none I had ever felt before. I figured, what else would he be besides evil, he was a friend of Herman.

Chapter 7

I was able to get away from the house, when Herman would leave for days at a time. Charles and I had known each other for a long time. He stayed away from me because he knew getting too close would cause me to be physically assaulted. Being with him was worth every risk taken. It was like a breath of fresh air. He was kind and gentle. He held me and treated me like I was a tender jewel. Soon after we had been seeing each other I became pregnant with my fourth child. Revealing that knowledge was a conversation I'll never forget. We were sitting in the dining room at the Pink House. Charles sat at the table looking at me.

"What did you just say," he asked with emotions ranging between excitement and fear.

"I'm pregnant. From the time of my last menstrual that would make you the father." I said softly with my head down.

Still Standing

"Pick your head up Verna. I told you to never talk to me with your head down. I like to see your face and your eyes when you talk to me." He touched my hand with one hand and the other he lifted my chin. "What are we going to do? He asked with true concern.

"We're not going to do anything!" I said, too loudly and too harshly. "I'm going to have this baby like I did before." I knew what he wanted, but I couldn't do it, I was too afraid. I held his hand tightly. "Charles, Herman has beat me for years saying that there was someone else when there wasn't. If he so much as thought we'd been together and this is your baby he'd kill all three of us. You can't say anything, you just can't." I spoke softly but he knew I was afraid, I was shaking all over just thinking about what would happen. We agreed to not mention it again, he would always be close enough to see his child.

By now I was allowed to attend church without having to fight with Herman about why I was going.

"Don't nobody want you with all these damn kids anyway. Go on to church if that's what make you happy!" He didn't understand, without God I would have checked out a long time ago. God and God alone would keep me strong on this journey of abuse and hardship.

On September 8th I gave birth to another beautiful baby girl. From the first time I held her she reminded me of my sister. I smiled down at her, "Your name is Beulah. I named you after your aunt." She lay there sleeping in my arms. I couldn't believe she weighed so much, 9lbs and 5ozs. Like Lolita and Myranda she had a head full of thick coal black, wavy hair. Her skin was the color of caramel candy, just like her sisters. God had blessed me with three of His little angels. I guess it was His way of letting me know He had not forgotten me.

A week after coming home from the hospital with Beulah, Bobby Sr. stopped by to visit us. He picked up the baby. "I see why you named her Beulah, she's beautiful like your sister," he said as he smiled down at her.

"Yes, it was something about the way she seemed to look at me when I first held her. I knew that would be her name."

Bobby put Beulah down and sat in the chair across the room. "What's wrong?" I asked, I could see something was bothering him.

"Tit and Bubba are gone," Those are the nicknames we had given the twins when we were children. "They left a few months ago and I thought they were with you."

"Herman brought Tit by to see me and Myranda a few weeks ago. He told me you knew she was with him. I thought he took her back home." Bobby shook his head. We both knew something wasn't right, we just didn't know what nor what we could do about it.

Once again I found myself pregnant soon after giving birth. Saying no to Herman was not an option. The one time I tried, he almost beat me to death. He didn't care that I was still healing, after recently having another vaginal birth, nor did he care that sex was very painful. I learned to lay there, be quiet, and thank God it never lasted long. The cheating and abuse was now happening during my pregnancies.

Herman was lying in bed one afternoon. He was still trying to get over a hangover from drinking and being with one of his other women the night before. The girls were playing on the floor while I sat there next to them. I was in my third trimester and it was more comfortable sitting on the floor than constantly bending over. They were happy babies. Lolita and Myranda were excited that Beulah was learning to smile and recognize them. Herman got out of bed, came into the living room and slapped me across the face. My first instinct was to block the children from his rage.

"I told you I had a damn headache and you sit your sorry ass down in front of the door and let these kids keep up all that noise!" He grabbed me and tried pushing me out of the way to get to the girls. He had begun to spank them.

"I'll keep them quiet, I promise! Please Herman, don't spank them!" I begged. He hit me again,

"Do something with them! If I come back in here I'm going to beat the hell out of you and those got damned babies!" he yelled and went back to lay down. I picked Beulah up and took the other two by the hand into the kitchen. I fixed them something to eat while I got a cold towel for the bruise on my face. Thank God, Bomb was gone with Alex so he wouldn't have to see his father hit me.

◊ ◊ ◊ ◊ ◊

When Beulah was about three months old, Herman and Earl burst through the door one night with Tit in tow. Earl pushed her towards me on the sofa and went into the bedroom with Herman and slammed the door.

"What are you doing with them? Where have you been, Bobby has been looking for you!" I had more questions, but stopped when I looked down in her face. I could see a handprint across the side of her face. She looked terrified. "Did Earl do this to you?" I whispered. She nodded her head yes. "Tit go back to Bobby before Earl hurts you. He's mean, Tit, he's evil."

"I can't go back to Bobby's. I'm pregnant, Earl got me pregnant." We both sat there with tears streaming down our faces.

"Bobby won't care, he'll take care of you and the baby, I know he will," I pleaded with her.

"I can't go back. They won't let me go back." She was so scared she was shaking.

"Who won't let you go back? What did Herman and Earl say to you?" She kept shaking her head. "Tell me so I can get you some help. Tit, Bobby will help you." Before she could say anything else the bedroom door opened and both men walked out.

"What are you telling her?" Earl yelled and pulled her away from me.

"Nothing, I didn't say anything!" I watched my sister cower in fear. "Tell him Verna Dean, I didn't say anything." When she looked at me my heart dropped. "No, she only told me she was pregnant and she was scared of being a mom so young. She said she doesn't know how to take care of a baby," I said, hoping they believed me.

"Come with me." Earl grabbed Tit by the arm and pulled her out the door. I'm not sure what kind of punishment Tit had to endure that night. I was scared for both my sister and myself. It was a while before she was allowed to come over again.

◊ ◊ ◊ ◊ ◊

The year 1963 was not like the others. Herman's abuse had subsided a little. Tit came by more often, but still wouldn't tell me what Herman and Earl did, or said to make her leave the safety and comfort of home. She would become instantly terrified whenever I brought it up so I stopped asking. That was a secret she took to her grave. We were both pregnant and stuck with abusive men who seemed like they came from the very pits of hell. They allowed us to spend time together, but we had to stay in the house. Except on Sundays, when we were allowed to go to church, and to the Pink House, to cook and clean. We didn't mind much, as long as we were together.

On May 17th Tit gave birth to a healthy, beautiful baby girl. She named her Gwendolyn Diane Martin. That was the day I found out Earl's last name. I didn't know it and was too afraid to ask. For some reason I didn't think Tit even knew his last name until that day. She didn't come back to my house after she and Gwen left the hospital and Herman wouldn't tell me where she lived. So, I waited until Earl would let her come by to visit. I just prayed it would be soon.

On September 11th I gave birth to a baby boy. He was smaller than his sisters. He had a head full of thick wavy hair and his skin was smooth as silk, and the color of rich dark chocolate. "Hi son, your name is Donald, Donald Ray Hall." He lay there looking at me with those beautiful brown eyes. "I guess you approve," I said smiling down at him.

Chapter 8

Herman stayed away from home a lot after Donald was born. The loves of his life consisted of fighting, drinking, and chasing women. I don't know if he beat any of his other women. Actually, I really didn't care as long as it kept him away from me and my children for as long as possible.

Because Herman was gone a lot I didn't get pregnant again right away. I got to enjoy playing, wrestling, and running with the kids without a big stomach in the way or always being so tired. We got to know what it felt like to be a family without the fear of being hit on or cursed out every time we laughed out loud or ran around the house.

Christmas came and went. The children had a nice and peaceful holiday. Tit and Gwen spent a lot of time with us. We were a family again, just larger. It was great being able to play with the kids and their new toys. I wonder how we ended up with toys that made so much noise. It seemed the more noise it made the more the kids liked playing with it. We welcomed a new year in, watching and praying over our children.

In February of 1964 the peace and quiet came to a screeching halt when Earl came into the house around 3:00am. I heard Tit screaming so I got out of bed and ran into the living room. She was on the sofa curled in a fetal position. I ran over to her and she practically climbed into my lap. She was shaking so bad. I held her, rocked her, and rubbed her back.

"I'm here Tit," I kept saying to calm her. She kept shaking her head.

"He's going to get me, Verna Dean," she whispered over and over. Herman walked in and closed the door behind him. He stared at me so hard, I got scared, but I wouldn't let my sister go. After a few minutes passed Herman told me, with venom in his voice, "Go in the room!"

I knew I risked getting beat, but I told him, "No, I'm staying with my sister."

He grabbed me by the hair and tried to pull me away, but Tit and I held on to each other even tighter.

Earl looked at us and laughed. "Let her stay. She can watch me beat Clara's ass for not doing what I told her."

Tit cried harder. "Verna Dean, go in the room. Please go in the room" she pleaded with me.

"No, it's too damn late now. Herman go get me a belt." Earl laughed, but in his eyes was anger and pure evil.

Herman laughed, "Next time both of y'all sorry asses will do what you're told!" He stepped in the bedroom and came out with his leather cowboy belt.

"What are you going to do with that?" I asked, afraid for me and Tit.

"This is what happens when she doesn't do what I tell her to do!"

I was no match for Earl's strength as he pulled my sister out of my arms and began beating her with that belt. Because she was so little he picked her up like a kid and hit her, over and over again. Each time that belt hit her skin it welted up or tore open. I tried to hide my face from the beating, but Herman slapped my hands down, grabbed my head and made me watch. Each time I tried to cover my ears he hit me and made me put them down. She sounded like a wounded animal caught in a trap. Earl dropped her to the floor but kept beating her. She couldn't scream anymore so she just lay there as he continued to beat her. He beat her so bad he left bruises on her that were there till the day she died.

When Earl turned towards me I didn't flinch. I looked at my sister curled in a ball, bleeding, then I looked back at him. I was angrier than I had ever been in my life. For a moment I wasn't even afraid of Herman. I pulled away from him and went to my sister. She knew I was there, but was too afraid to move. I turned and looked at both of them. I guess they knew, at that moment, if either one of them came close to either of us somebody was going to die that night. I pulled her into my arms. "Come on, I got you, he won't touch you again tonight." They looked at me and left out the door cursing.

I took her into the bedroom and pulled off what was left of her shirt. She winced from the pain. She took my hand, "Verna Dean, I tried. I tried to do everything he told me."

I looked at her, "Is this the first time he's whipped you with a belt?"

"No, but it's never been this bad before," she talked in a whisper as she cried into the pillow.

"Shhhhh, lay still while I clean you up." I kept caressing her face so she could calm down. "I love you Tit. I'll protect you from them tonight," I said softly to her.

"He took Gwen. I don't know where my baby is. He won't give me my baby," she cried.

"We'll find her and get her back," I promised. That calmed her down.

I gave her one of my pain pills and soon she was off to sleep. Ms. Dora, our neighbor who lived across the street, was a nurse. I went and got her to come and tend to Tit's back. It was too much for me to look at, so I turned away as tears rolled down my face. I could hear Tit wince from the pain even as she slept. Ms. Dora put medicine on her back and dressed it. When she finished I helped her get Tit comfortable, so she wouldn't roll over on her back. I kept thinking, *whatever it was he wanted her to do, it didn't require him beating her half to death with a belt.* Ms. Dora gave me instructions on how to care for my sister's back.

"Verna Dean, you should call the police and get out of here before those crazy ass men kill one of y'all," she pleaded with me before she left.

"How can I call the police when half of the force is his friends, and the other half is scared shitless of him? It'll just make it worse." I walked her to the bottom of the steps.

She turned to look at me, "He beat her really

bad. You have to keep her back clean and dressed at all times. It's gonna hurt for a few days, but it'll get better." I thanked her and gave her a hug. "I'll check on Tit in a few days," she said with compassion. She hugged me again and crossed the street to her house. I stood there for a moment and went back upstairs. Tit and all the kids were able to sleep, but I couldn't, as I kept watch over my family.

◊ ◊ ◊ ◊ ◊

By the time of Donald's first birthday I was five months pregnant again. I'll be 23 years old in October with five kids and one on the way. More than once I wondered, *how in God's name, did I get here, living this life of fear and abuse, not just for me, but for my children.*

Chapter 9

I got sick again and was admitted back into the hospital when I was seven months pregnant. I was there when my youngest child was born. On January 8, 1965 Albert Lee Hall was born. He was a healthy baby. He weighed 11 lbs. and 2ozs. He would drink an 8oz bottle of milk and scream to the top of his lungs. The nursery started putting pablum (today's rice cereal) in his milk when he was three days old. He never used a 4oz bottle for anything but water.

After a few days I noticed the other mothers had their new babies in the room with them, but I didn't have mine. I was concerned so I stopped the day nurse. "Where is my son? Is he ok? I see all the other babies, why can't I have mine?" I asked her.

She looked me in the eyes with a straight face and told me, "We're watching him in the nursery because we found a rash on him."

Still Standing

"A rash? Is it bad? Where is it and how did it get there?" I kept asking questions, but she would only say, that the doctor would talk to me when he got in.

When the head nurse came by to check on me she didn't seemed concerned about anything, so I asked her, "Is my son okay? Did you all find out what caused the rash on him?"

She shook her head, "Mrs. Hall one of the nurses told you a fib. Your son is fine. He's the biggest baby we've had to be born here and the nurses seem to be taking turns holding him and feeding him. I'll have one of the nurses bring him over right away. I'm sorry they had you worried for nothing." We both laughed as she walked out the door. She was laughing but somebody got in trouble for telling that lie. Albert went home in 6-9 month clothes. I looked at all the newborn outfits, shook my head, and gave them away.

When I got home from the hospital with Albert, Herman was there waiting for me. He made me change the sheets and covers on the bed so he and his girlfriend could sleep there. Albert and I slept on the couch. I still had to cook, clean, and take care of the kids, plus a new baby, while she ate, drank, and laid up in my bed. Once Mother McGowen found out what was going on, she stepped in and put a stop to it. Mother, as she was affectionately known, lived in the

Pink House and was pastor of McGowen Memorial Church, where we attended. She was quite the force to be reckoned with. For some reason, when she spoke, Herman listened, even if I had to pay for it later. She made both of them leave but I knew, from the look Herman gave me on his way out I was going to get a beating when he came back. At the time I didn't care, I needed the break from him, his alcohol, and his fist.

Chapter 10

By the time Albert turned two years old I started having trouble with my right foot. It started swelling. I couldn't figure out anything that I had done to it so Herman thought I was lying.

"Yo ass just lazy and don't want to take care of these kids," he would yell at me.

In the meantime it got to the point where the pain was getting so bad I couldn't walk. I had to crawl around the house to take care of the kids and Herman still wouldn't let me go to the doctor. Inspite of the pain I cooked everyday so my kids would never miss a meal. Also I kept them neat and clean. When Mother found out about my foot she came around to the house with the pistol that she always kept in her apron pocket and told Herman to leave. Once he left she had one of the young men from the church to come upstairs and pack me to the car so I could go to the hospital

They admitted me into Hermann Hospital where I stayed for seven months. My children were taken care of by Ms. Hazel and other ladies from the church. One of my friends had a beauty salon across the street from our house. She kept my daughters hair pressed, combed, and looking pretty.

The doctors at Hermann Hospital couldn't figure out what was going on with my foot so I was sent to John Sealy Hospital in Galveston, Texas to see a podiatry specialist. After a few weeks of being in John Sealy my foot had swollen up so big it literally burst open at my ankle. You could see where my ankle and my foot bone connected together. When the doctors took x-rays, it showed my entire right foot was infected. The infection had softened my bones to the texture of corn meal. I had been in the hospital four months when Alex brought Donald and Albert to see me. It hurt that they had a hard time remembering me.

Alex gave me a hug and told me, "Remember they are only babies. They'll remember when you come home."

His words comforted me. At two and three years old, I guess it would be easy to forget who I was.

Then Donald hugged me and said, "I love you mama." Albert did too, but I think he only did what he saw his brother do. It didn't matter, it still made me

Still Standing

feel a little better.

After six and a half months of trying to strengthen my bones at John Sealy, the doctors decided to run a few more tests. After all those test were done and the specialists saw no change, they said amputation of my entire right foot was their only option. I was 25 years old with six kids, no high school diploma, an abusive husband, and now I was facing the possibility of losing my foot. I did the only thing I knew to do, talk to my Father. I lay there in pain looking up to God. With tears running down my face I could only say three words, "Lord, help me."

The night before I was scheduled to go into surgery my pastor, Rev. Charles Turner came to visit me. He taped a piece of paper over the hospital bandages on my ankle and prayed for me.

"Hold on, you may have a rough night, but everything is going to be alright," he told me as he held my hand. I looked into the eyes that I trusted and nodded my head. He kissed me on my forehead and then softly on the lips. "I'll be here to pick you up in the morning."

"I can't go home right after having this kind of surgery. Plus I won't have but one foot," I said as I begin to cry.

"Don't cry Verna, it's going to be ok, I promise. Mother told me to tell you, you're healed." He fluffed my pillow and pulled the cover over my shoulders. He left saying, "I will see you in the morning."

I lay there thinking, *Mother said I'm healed.* I had seen her pray over and heal others so I took comfort in that.

Later that night I tried to sleep, but I couldn't because the pain was overwhelming. It was a different type of pain. The throbbing stopped and the pain seemed to engulf my entire foot. Around midnight the pain was so great I could feel my body shaking, but I couldn't say anything or call for a nurse. Now my cry was, "Lord, my Father, help me through this pain." About 3:30am the pain started to subside. I was finally able to rest. I soon realized there was no more pain. I drifted off into a deep sleep. I was awakened the next morning by the doctors coming to get me ready for surgery.

They asked, how I had slept. I told them how much pain I had experienced through the night.

I told them, how the pain was so bad, then stopped right after 3:00am."

They removed the paper that was taped to my

bandage and examined my foot. When they saw the swelling had gone down, the specialist had x-rays ordered right away. The doctors came back after checking the x-rays and took the bandages off of my ankle. They asked me, what I had done to my ankle and how the paper got taped on to my bandages.

I told them about Rev. Turner's visit, how he taped the paper to my foot and prayed over it. I could see the weird look on their faces. "What's wrong? What happened to my foot? Why did the pain stop?" I kept asking questions that they couldn't answer. They were looking at me crazy and I was looking at them just as crazy. Then I remembered Rev.'s last words on his way out the door, *Mother said I was healed.* It was then that I realized all the pain I was going through was a healing process.

Before I knew it, it seemed like every doctor on that floor was in my room. They all looked at the x-rays and then at my foot and ankle. The spot on my ankle had completely closed up except for a little dime sized hole, for the rest of the infection to drain. My bones were solid again! The doctors said they didn't know what happened, I wouldn't need the surgery, but I would walk with a limp for the rest of my life, and I would have to use crutches for at least six months. There was no reason to keep me any longer so the nurses did my paperwork for me to be discharged. By the time they were completed Rev. walked in and ask me if I was ready to go home. He shook hands with all of the doctors, got my paperwork, and wheeled me out of the hospital. After two weeks at home I was able to go to church. I walked in and gave my crutches to the usher. I didn't need them anymore and I never walked with a limp.

Chapter 11

Once I got home and my foot didn't give me anymore trouble I started working. I worked doing what I did best, house cleaning. I made $11.00 a day working three days a week. Sometimes I rode three or four different buses to get to work. I had to always rush home because if I didn't get there at a certain time Herman would say I was meeting somebody. You would think he'd let Alex or someone give me a ride so he wouldn't have to worry about that, but he was too mean and evil to even allow that.

Herman's abuse didn't stop. He had never acknowledged God's presence before, so to say he saw my healing as a miracle is by far a stretch of the imagination. Therefore, he still didn't like me going or taking the children to church. One Sunday morning as I was coming out of the door of the church he snatched me and began slapping me across my face. I could hear my children screaming and crying. He heard them too, but it didn't stop him from hitting me. Even though he was drunk and could have been easily overtaken no one was going to help me or say anything because they were all too afraid of him. It took Mother to come and stand at the doorway for him to push me down and walk away. "Get her and take her into my office," she said with authority, but to no one in particular. Alex and Pookie (a dear friend of mine,) picked me up and took me to the back to clean my face and help fix my clothes. Some of the other ladies took the kids back into the church to calm them down. When the children had to witness his abuse they were never okay until they could be with me to make sure I was alright. I kept thinking *they're too young to have to keep seeing this over and over.* Mother came into her office. She didn't have to say anything, everyone knew to leave us alone.

"I'll go feed the kids," Pookie said over her shoulder as she walked out.

"How are you?" Mother asked. She took out a bottle of blessed oil, put some across my forehead and prayed for me. When she prayed her voice had a way of soothing the soul of its troubles. After she prayed aloud she just held my hands for a moment. I know she was saying something. To whom I don't know, I just figured she was calling on God to protect me.

Still Standing

The beatings had gotten so bad at one time that Mother was afraid for me and the kids so she hid us out. We were right down the street but he couldn't find us for a while. Once he found out where we were, he told me if we came home he would never hit me or the kids again. He had never made that promise before so I got the kids together and we went home. He was nice for a week, maybe even two weeks. It started off with a push or shove one day. Then it gradually ended up to the same abuse as before.

There was a café down the street from where we lived named The Hawaiian Eye. One night Herman wanted me to go there with him. He knew I hated places like that, but saying no wasn't an option with him. He tried to introduce me to one of his friends. I didn't want to shake hands with him because, I knew Herman's temper, and I would be accused of something. It would be, I held his hand too long or if I didn't shake his hand then I thought I was too good to shake his friend's hand. Once his friend smiled at me I knew, from the look on Herman's face, what was going to happen when we got home. And it did.

◊ ◊ ◊ ◊ ◊

One night Herman got into a fight and came home to get his shot gun. I tried to stop him, but one of the barrels went off. I ended up getting buck shots everywhere. I was rushed to Ben Taub Hospital. The doctors spent quite a while picking buck shots out of my face, neck, and breast. I was blessed that none of them hit me in the eyes. I still have some in my breast and neck. Every time I have chest x-rays or a mammogram done I have to let them know that they are there.

◊ ◊ ◊ ◊ ◊

After years of abuse one day I decided I couldn't take it anymore. I figured Herman wouldn't want the children and they would be given homes where there was love and peace, without the abuse. I washed and combed the girls' hair and gave all the kids a bath. I cooked and fed them and put them to bed. I took a bath and got every pill I had and took them all. I had 11 valiums and some other type of pain pill. This night, of all nights my sister-in-law came by. She rarely left Angleton and visited unexpectedly. I was rushed to the hospital where they pumped out my stomach. I wasn't myself for two days. I don't remember anything, but I was told I went off on a lot of people. Because I was always quiet and kept a lot of things to myself I told everyone off that had done anything to me or my kids. Well, I guess I let it all hang out!

After the suicide episode Herman didn't fight

Still Standing

me or beat the kids as much, for a while, anyway. The kids were getting older so they could go outside to play on the porch. The entire yard was fenced in and they knew not to touch the latch on the gate. Being outside helped keep them out of Herman's way during the daytime. Beulah and Donald were allowed to play across the street at the Bilton's home. Mrs. Barbara would let the kids come over and play on their outdoor gym called a Whirly Bird. They would have so much fun I could hear them laughing across the street. I didn't understand how being spent around until you're dizzy was so much fun. Albert was still too young to be downstairs, so he stayed in the kitchen with me most of the time as I prepared lunch and/or dinner. I sat him on the table so he could see everything. He became my official taste tester. He would get so excited when I let him stir something in a bowl. He would make a mess, but seeing him laugh and eat more than he stirred was worth it. It was the quiet times like these that I enjoyed most. It didn't take much to make my kids laugh and be happy. Whenever Herman and Earl stayed away for days or weeks at a time, we didn't ask questions, we didn't look for them, we just enjoyed being a peaceful family with Tit and her children.

Chapter 12

One night after I had fed the kids, bathe them, and put them to bed Herman came in drunk. He had enough food to feed the neighborhood.

"Wake the kids up so they can eat!" he yelled.

"They already ate. They're asleep," I said softly from across the room.

"Wake them up! I bought this for them to eat!" Of course my word meant nothing, so he woke the kids up, made them get to the table, and then got angry because they wouldn't eat. "Stupid bitch, you trying to turn my kids against me?"

"No, it's after midnight and they're full and tired." I tried to explain. He wasn't hearing it. He pulled off his belt and began whipping them. I noticed Randy (Myranda) wouldn't cry. Herman kept hitting her, but she would not cry. He finally left her sitting at the table. She bucked her eyes, and I could see her

Still Standing

huffing and puffing. I kept praying Herman wouldn't turn around and see her looking at him the way she was. All I could think at that time was, *oh Lord, this child has that Hall temper like her daddy!*

There was another time after a lot of abuse. I thought I would try to commit suicide again. Tit and her children were living with us at the time. Herman left his shot gun on the dresser. I picked up the shot gun and went in the bathroom. I put the gun up to my head and tried to pull the trigger, but it wouldn't do anything, My sister kept hearing the click, click, from me cocking the gun and came into the bathroom.

She stood there with tears running down her face. "You can't leave me and the kids here alone Verna Dean."

"I can't take this anymore," I cried softly.

"I know it's hard. It's hard for me too. I need you, the kids need you." I stood looking at her and tried to pull the trigger again. Darn thing still wouldn't go off. Tit walked over to me and easily took the shot gun out of my hand. When she did it went off, with the bullet hitting the ceiling. I was so angry because it wouldn't go off for me. Tit put the gun back in the room, on the dresser. We sat on the sofa for the remainder of the night. We didn't say anything to each other. We just held each other tightly and silently thanked God that He kept the gun from going off.

A few weeks after my second attempt at suicide Herman's father, Taylor Hall, came to Houston and tried to take me and the kids to Angleton, TX with him. I heard him fussing with Herman but couldn't make out what they were saying. Herman wouldn't allow us to go. He stayed for a while and played with the kids. When it was time for Taylor to leave he hugged each of his grandkids. He hugged me, told me to be careful, and left.

◊ ◊ ◊ ◊ ◊

On Halloween night of 1969, Herman came home drunk as usual, but this night he walked in, in a full blown rage. He began beating me. Lolita and Beulah started screaming and trying to pull him off of me.

"Stop! Stop! Stop hitting my mama!"

I could hear them screaming, but couldn't get to them. Herman hit me with something, I couldn't tell at the time but it left me half dazed. "No, no, go to your room," I kept saying, but with them screaming and Herman yelling, they couldn't hear me. When Herman turned towards me I saw pure evil in his eyes. He picked up one of his leather belts and began to beat the girls. Randy sat in the window of the living room looking into my bedroom with her eyes bucked and a look of hatred on her face. I could see her little hands balled into fists. I don't know if God was answering my prayer or if my pure will made her remain on that window seat.

Donald and Albert were in their bedroom. They did what I taught them to do when Herman came home in a rage. "Get behind the foot of the bed, pull the cover over you, and don't say a word, just sit as still as possible." They didn't understand at first, but after a few years of his consistent outburst and whippings, they learned the drill down pact.

Herman came back into the room and beat me again. He sat on the bed and glanced in the corner. Beulah was crouched down between the dresser and the closet. I don't know when she came back in, but there she was. *Please God, don't let him whip her again.* My prayer was answered because Herman didn't go after her. He reached over on the side of the bed and pulled out his shot gun. He then reached into the night stand and came out with six bullets. He pulled me by my hair and looked me in the face.

"I'm sick of you and these got damned kids. These are for y'all." He rolled the bullets in his hand. "I have one for each of these noisy ass kids. I'm going to make you watch as I shoot their asses one by one. Then this last one right here is for you!" He held the last bullet to my face. He pushed me on the floor and went and laid down. "When I wake up, you and those damn kids are dead!"

I got up off the floor and went to check on the other kids. Randy was still sitting on the window seat. I remember looking at her and she looked at me and then in the room at Herman. I don't know what it was that I saw in her eyes. Neither one of us said anything. She saw Herman beat me, but I wondered if she heard any of what he said. I went into the kids' room. Don and Al were still where I had taught them to be. I put them to bed and kissed them. Lolita was fast asleep. I kissed her too and left the room. I went into the bathroom and gathered every pill in the cabinet. I went back into my bedroom and picked up all my pills I had on the dresser. I took 54 valiums and 15 of another pain pill, and everything that was over the counter as well. I then sat on side of the bed and watched Herman sleep. I looked over at Randy, still sitting on the window seat, and Beulah crouching in the corner and my heart hurt for them. The pills started kicking in and I began to drift in and out, but I kept what focus I could on Herman and his shot gun.

After a while Herman started waking up. The first thing he did was reach for his shot gun. Afraid for the life of my children and myself, I beat him to the gun. I stood in front of him, loaded and cocked the gun, click, click, I pulled the trigger, boom. He fell

Still Standing

back on the bed. He came up. I didn't know if it was from the force of the shot or he did it on his own. Out of fear and full of pills I cocked the gun again, click, click, I pulled the trigger, boom. He fell back on the bed, but didn't get up this time. Blood covered his chest and bed. I stood there for a moment, set the gun on the bed, then sat there also. I remember hearing someone come through the window from on top of the garage. I think it was my brother, Bubba. I barely recognized his face. I was going under from the pills. I don't know how much time lapsed before Bubba went back out the window and Alex came over. I somewhat remember one policeman covering Herman with a sheet and another one leading me outside. I sat in the police car wondering what was going on. There were so many lights, and policemen were everywhere. I think I saw Ms. Dora and Mrs. Barbara with my children. I don't know who went where, I let the pills do what they were taken to do, I laid back on the seat and everything went black.

The first thing I remember was being in a room eating a bologna sandwich. I don't know if it was the police station or the hospital, after getting my stomach pumped again. I vaguely remember the police asking me what happened. I think I was able to explain to them what happened and that Herman wouldn't let us

66

leave with his dad. I was going in and out of consciousness again so I don't remember the details of what I told them, but it's all on public file somewhere at the police station. When I became fully awake I was at home with my children. For the first time in a very long time I felt a sense of peace and calm. I was thankful his family handled all of the funeral arrangements. I had no idea what funeral insurance was or if he had any. We buried Herman the second weekend of November. I remember crying and being escorted out of the church. I don't know what I felt that day as they lowered his body in the grave. I would be lying if I said some of those feelings weren't feelings of relief. I wouldn't have to fear for my life nor my children's ever again.

◊ ◊ ◊ ◊ ◊

Now, I was looking at going to court facing a judge. I knew even if I had to do time in jail my kids wouldn't have to face the fear of seeing their mom ever being hit again. They gave us a court date and told me Myranda and Beulah had to appear in court also. We went to court. I was so proud of my little girls. They didn't appear to be afraid. They told their account of what they saw. Myranda had seen so much. The judge sentenced me to three years of probation. After eighteen months the courts terminated the sentence. Tit and her children moved in with me. We

Still Standing

didn't hear from Earl any more once Herman was buried. We found out later he and some other guy had tied themselves together and decided to see who could take the most bullets before they died. Well, needless to say they are both dead. We were free to be a family, a family without fear of hurt and abuse.

Chapter 13

There I was 27 years old, a single mother with six children. I was still working for $11.00 a day. Thankfully Mrs. Rose asked could I work an extra day. It wasn't much, but I knew I could make it, failing was not an option with six little people totally dependent on me. I learned to sew in homemaking class while in school, therefore I made most of my kids' clothes, even the boys. I started sewing for other people which brought in more money than cleaning houses. I worked and took care of my children, but I still couldn't find true peace until I moved out of that apartment. It held so many painful memories. I sat down one evening with Pookie and told her I was ready to get out of Third Ward. She gave me some leads to look into for houses. I knew it was time to leave all of this behind me and never look back.

We moved to South Park on Doulton Street. The children were so excited, it was their first time living in a house, our house. For a while the children

Still Standing

and I would catch the bus on Sundays to Third Ward for church. Catching three buses every Sunday going to church and three coming home, if we couldn't find a way, had become pretty taxing. Beulah started going to the church across the street, Greater Saint Matthew. She liked it a lot and wanted to sing in the choir for children her age, The Little Angels. She talked about the little green capes they got to wear. She came home the first Sunday in June of 1971 and told me she joined church and they were getting ready for Vacation Bible School. The next Sunday all the kids and I got up and got dressed, instead of going to the bus stop we walked across the street to church. The service was spirit filled and very uplifting. It had been a very long time since I walked out of church with a feeling of hope. I knew I would be coming back as I walked home.

Beulah was very excited about Greater Saint Matthew. I was okay with her excitement until she came home asking to go on a trip with the church. I had attended a few times but didn't know anyone. The youth were going to Six Flags over Texas in Fort Worth and she wanted to go. I had never let any of my kids go so far without me. I'll never forget walking over to the church with her lunch and First Lady, Theola Booker greeted me. I explained that Beulah had never been that far away from home and I was nervous about letting her go. She promised me that she would take care of her. It was something about her gentle spirit that let me know my daughter would be safe in her care. I told Beulah she could go, she grabbed her lunch, kissed me and ran to get on the bus.

A few months later my family and I joined Greater Saint Matthew. Pastor and Sis. Booker welcomed us as if they had known us all of their lives. The entire church congregation was like one big happy family. They were always ready to lend a helping hand. It was here that I began to search for more of God. I knew He had kept me all of those years and now I was ready to devote the rest of my life to Him, and I knew this was the church where I would serve. I joined the Mission Board, worked with the youth ministry, and sang with the Senior Choir. Lolita and Myranda joined the Young Adult Choir. Oh my God, that choir could sing! Beulah, of course got to wear her green cape as she sang with the Little Angels Choir. The boys didn't want to sing, but they enjoyed sitting in church watching us. It was great to see my children enjoying life as children should. They were able to attend church without fear of me being jumped on, or them being hit or spanked.

I watched as the kids began to make friends. They would play ball in the street or sit outside on the driveway and laugh. What a wonderful sound, hearing my children laugh. We had a big back yard so they would play volleyball, badminton, and horseshoes. Keeping them off of the pear tree until they ripened is another story, filled with stomach aches, tears, Pepto Bismol, and toilet paper.

I began making friends of my own at church and in the neighborhood. After living next to an empty house for about three or four months we got new neighbors. Blanche was a single mother with three beautiful girls. Our families instantly became good friends. She liked to party and have fun. So it became her mission to help me loosen up and join the party. Blanche took me to the store and bought me a pack of Camel cigarettes, a lighter, and a cigarette case. I wanted to look grown, so she told me to get something to drink. I saw a pretty blue can with a silver bull on it. It was cute so I got it. When the kids saw it they laughed at me. "We'll be waiting for you to come home," Bomb said. Then all the kids started laughing again. I should have known something wasn't right then.

I went over to Blanche's with my blue can and cigarette pouch. I watched them swirl the smoke from their cigarettes. I couldn't figure out how they did it. "You swallow the smoke then blow it out," one of them said. Well, I swallowed the smoke and dang near coughed my lungs out of my body. I thought the coughing made me a little light headed so I got my can of pretty blue beer and drank some of it. By the time I got to half a can Blanche and one of the guys had to help me get home. I was laughing about everything and talking about nothing, but doing a lot of it. I remember the girls putting me in a cold shower to help sober me up. I stepped out of the shower and went straight for the toilet. I felt like I was throwing up my insides. I had a hangover for a couple of days. When I did sober up, my kids had a good laugh at my expense. "Thought you were grown huh?" they teased. Well, that was it for my life of partying, cigarettes, and beer. That was my adventure at trying something that I knew would never happen again. At least I can say, I tried."

Chapter 14

Times got hard with me not having a high school diploma to get a good job. Making $44 a week plus odd jobs in sewing wasn't enough to keep the bills paid. School was getting ready to start and I had no idea how I was going to get all the kids' stuff for school, pay bills, and rent. A friend of mine named Phillip told me to bring the kids to a local shoe store (I can't remember the name). I kinda argued with him for a moment telling him I didn't have the money. "Verna, will you just bring them like I asked you to?" He said it so nicely that I got the kids together and took them to the store. I stood and watched as he measured each of the children's feet. He went to the back and came out with two bags for each of the kids. They were given a pair of tennis shoes for school, and loafers that could be worn to school or church.

He pulled me to the side and wiped the tears from my face. "I'm manager and part owner." He smiled at me.

"Why?" I asked.

"Because I like you." He smiled at me and took my hand. "You're a wonderful mother and you do such a great job with your children"

"Thank you." I smiled back at him. "I have to get the kids home and ready for dinner."

"Okay, I hope to see you again." He let my hand fall to my side and walked us all to the door. "Enjoy your shoes," he said to the kids as they walked out the door. That night I cried myself to sleep giving praise to God for providing for me, especially when I didn't even see a way possible. Phillip started visiting. He later took me shopping to get the kids' school supplies and clothes.

Phillip and I dated for over a year and a half. We had great times together. So many times I would smile and think, *so this is what it feels like to date a man that respects and treats me like a lady.* I smiled and laughed a lot with him. He had a witty sense of humor and it seemed like it gave him great pleasure to hear me laugh. He was tall, a sharp dresser, and oh my gosh he was handsome. His skin was the color of milk chocolate and his hair was coal black, wavy, and soft. It felt odd, but wonderful, going out on dates to dinner and a movie. He enjoyed being around the kids as much he enjoyed being with me. Being with Phillip

Still Standing

made me so happy I decided to do something that I'd wanted to do again since I was a kid, grow a garden. I went to Kmart and bought a lot of rose bushes and gardening tools. We got stuck a lot, but me and my children had fun planting that rose garden. I love roses and soon the kids started teasing me saying, I treated my roses like part of the family. After a while Phillip started helping me take care of the garden. "Whatever makes you smile, I'm all in," he said each time he came over in old jeans to help.

I'll never forget the beautiful black baby dolls he bought Randy and Beulah for Christmas. I believe it was their first African American doll. They played with those dolls every day until Randy decided dolls weren't her thing anymore. I watched her become a tomboy right before my eyes. If I wasn't paying attention I would have missed it. It was like she switched overnight. Beulah didn't mind because that was an extra doll, and pots and pans she got to call her own.

Everything was going well until Phillip asked me to marry him. I couldn't do it, not after all that I had been through. That and he was younger than me, with no kids of his own. He kept saying that didn't matter, but I felt someday it would. I had to break it off which left me alone and feeling sad. I had gotten used to being treated as if I was beautiful and I knew I was going to miss it.

◇ ◇ ◇ ◇ ◇ ◇

After Phillip and I broke up, things were okay for a while, but life got rough again. I took part time jobs when and where I could. We had to move from Doulton Street to a house on Pershing. It was a nice house. The drive way had a steep slope to it, so the boys and Randy used it as a ramp to ride their Tonka trucks down. Don came in screaming one day, his truck had tipped over and he hit his face on the ground. It tore the skin off his chin. Randy stood there fussing as I cleaned him up, "I told him to hold the truck on both sides before he turn, but nawwww he had to show off." I looked at her and shook my head. "Randy stop fussing, he'll listen next time," I laughed at both of them. As soon as that bandage was on they were back on those trucks rolling down the drive way again. Lolita was in her room and Beulah was somewhere playing house with her dolls. They had no idea there was barely any food in the house or that all the bills had pink slips. They were happy, we were a family, and I was trusting God to feed us and provide for us.

One afternoon Randy came in the house yelling she could see a baby in the ditch behind our house. We all ran out to see what was going on. She kept pointing, "There, over there!" Tears started rolling down her face.

Still Standing

"I don't see anything. All I see is a doll right there," I pointed in the same direction.

"That's not a doll, that's the baby," she said softly.

"Oh my God!" Me, Beulah, and Lolita said at the same time. After a while the back part of the house was covered with policemen.   We all watched in stunned silence as they lifted the baby from the ditch and wrapped it in a white sheet.

Chapter 15

We moved a lot after leaving Pershing Street. It was hard, but it seemed like the more we struggled the tighter our bond became. As I sit here, I thank God the hard times didn't make my children bitter. They all seemed to have my loving and giving heart. After that they had their own personalities, and boy, were they different.

My oldest, Herman Jr picked up the nickname Bomb when he was a toddler. He loved loud noises and thought everyone else did too. By the time he was two years old every cake I made had dips and rolls from him beating on my pans. For his third birthday Mother bought him a Ludwig drum set. That became his passion and he was so good he was playing drums at church every Sunday by the age of five.

He was my disciplinarian for the younger kids. His hands were huge and worked better than any belt I could have bought. His siblings looked up to him even

Still Standing

when he began to make bad life choices. It seemed like overnight my son with the gentle spirit became hostile, bitter, and angry at the world. He started using drugs, and his life went downhill from there. He would go to prison for five or six years, come home and stay out about eight months to a year, then do something to get locked up again. He hated being incarcerated so I didn't understand why he did it over and over again. He was fighting demons that he wouldn't tell anyone about.

When Bomb was home the family flocked around him all the time. His sense of humor was still intact and he never learned to tell a joke without laughing before he finished it. He would pay a debt and ask to borrow $5 of what he'd just paid back. His love for his nieces and nephews was unquestionable. Beulah's sons and grandsons inherited his love for drums and every now and then you could see him stick his chest out with pride.

Lolita got her nickname, Neat, when she was young also. She was always cleaning and put things in place. She was quiet most of the time. She seemed to always sit back and survey everything going on. Lolita learned at an early age that she didn't like spankings, so she would tell me everything, everybody did when I was at work or church. Whenever I questioned the other kids about something they thought I had no idea about they would all turn to

Lolita.

I remember her first time cooking spaghetti. It was so bad the dogs wouldn't eat it. Her siblings got a good laugh then, but she shut them up rather quickly because she learned to cook and cook very well. She learned to braid hair at a very young age. She taught herself by practicing on her sister's head. By the time she was eleven years old she could braid hair better than anyone we knew. Her parts lived up to her name, Neat. She made some of the prettiest braid designs in her sister's hair.

Myranda got her nickname because most people pronounced her name, My-Randy, it became Randy for short. She had a bad temper that could go from 0 to 100 in less than a minute. She was the outspoken one. She felt she had to have the last word. I remember Herman would pop her and sometimes knock her down, but she would get up speaking her mind. So many times I would tell her, "Randy, just be quiet." She'd turn those big buckeyes on me and shake her head. When she was around five years old, one day she told me, "Mama, one day when I get big I'm going to kill my daddy for always hitting you and whipping us." I would try to talk those feelings out of her, but she would look at me, shake her head, and say, "Yep, I'm going to get him." Then I'd shake my head and leave her alone.

Still Standing

Beulah, was fun and loving, until you crossed her. She would curse you out and never give it a second thought. When asked, "Where did she get such a rough vocabulary?" I had to give credit to our Mina Bird, Tommy, and living by the Hawaiian Eye for so many years. The drunk guys going by our house used profanity like a second language. Beulah thought it was cool so it became her second language as well. The crazy part was, I never knew when someone would do or say something to get her tongue to going. It didn't matter how many whippings she got for cursing, it never took the edge off that sharp tongue of hers. Beulah also had a love for dolls. At one time she had so many they would creep me out. It didn't matter if their eyes, legs, or arms were missing she would still keep them and play with them like they were brand new. I got tired of trying to help her name them so I told her, "Lucy is a good name for all your dolls, then you'd never mix them up." Crazy as it sounds, it worked for her. I'm still shaking my head.

Donald, we only shortened his name to call him Don. He had dark chocolate skin like my dad. I don't know what happened but, he was kinda funny looking when he was younger, (thank God he outgrew those years.) When he looked into the mirror all he saw was a handsome prince. He didn't understand the crown was supposed to shine brightly, not him. He would rub lots of Vaseline on himself to keep from getting ashy, especially his face. I would always tell him, "Boy, you're shining like new money," or "Don, you have enough grease on your face to fry a chicken." For some reason those were compliments to him because he would smile so big all you could see were his white teeth.

Don would change clothes two and three times a day. I guess he got tired of me fussing about washing clothes he learned very early how to wash his own and iron them too.

Albert, I'm shaking my head just saying his name. It's always the baby that makes you wonder why you kept going. Albert didn't like going to school starting from kindergarten. I sent him off to school one morning with his siblings. I was going to the bus stop, but decided to take another route. There was my son, skipping school, sitting on a bridge swinging his legs while eating his lunch. He saw me and smiled. I calmly walked over to him, "Albert, why aren't you at school?"

"I wanted to eat my lunch and they said it wasn't time so I came here to eat," he batted those big brown eyes at me with a smile. Well, that was until I grabbed his butt up from there and took him back to school.

I'll share more about my children later. They

Still Standing

were always my inspiration to hold on. During the
times that had been so rough that I tried to take my
life, I'm glad God the Father saw fit to keep me here,
Still Standing.

Chapter 16

Today as I sit here, I realize Satan was out for me a long time ago. He tried to discredit God's love for me so many times in so many ways. I remember a time when we had no food in the house. Satan wanted me to blame God as we prepared to leave for church one Sunday evening. I told the kids to be sure to eat some of the snacks they had at church because that would be dinner for tonight.

After we got home, I told them all to go to bed so they wouldn't get too hungry again. Lolita had to wash her clothes for school on that Monday. She walked outside to the washing machine. I heard her drop the basket and start calling for me to come outside. I guess I wasn't moving fast enough, she came inside with tears in her eyes. "Mama, mama there's food in the washer and dryer."

"Girl, what are you talking about?" I asked, afraid to believe her.

Still Standing

"Neat, you're hungry and seeing things," Myranda and Beulah teased.

"No, come see. It's all kinds of food out there and sodas too." We all went to the door as she reached into the washer and came out with bottles of soda, several loaves of bread, and containers of barbeque sauce, beans and potato salad. "Get this!" she shouted at all of us to bring us out of the trance we were in. The girls were taking that in the house as she called for her brothers. Lolita opened the dryer and pulled out pans of sausage, ribs, and chicken. She reached in again and pulled out a brisket. We all came back out onto the porch looking around to see who left all the food.

My friend Sam called a few hours later and asked, "Has anyone been to the washer yet?"

"It was you?" I asked.

"Yes, my boss said he heard you, and for me to bring that over to the house."

"Tell your boss I said thank you and we appreciate it very much."

"Ok, tell the kids hello. Enjoy the food. I hope it was enough."

"It's more than enough. We'll be able to eat for

the rest of the week."

"Good," he said. "Y'all have a good evening," then he hung up the phone and was gone. I never saw him again after that. I kept wondering, *who is his boss? I never told anyone about my situation.* It took me a few days to realize who his boss was. The only thing I did prior to that Sunday was pray. God kept showing Himself strong not just on my behalf, but on behalf of my children.

In 1974 I met and married J.W. LaCour. I thought this would be it for me, love, loyalty, and the together forever thing. I had six kids and he had six, so our family grew really large rather quickly. Our families bonded right away. When his children would come to visit on weekends they never wanted to go home. Back then life was simple and a lot of the fun things to do were free. We would pack a big lunch, park by Hobby Airport, and watch the planes land and take off. We would eat, laugh, and play games around the car. Back then it was also cool to lay on top of the car and star gaze.

We attended church together as a family. We were active with the youth department. J.W. was soon ordained as a minister. I was so proud of him. We christened our first godchild, LaVelle Martin.

Still Standing

Everyone teased him because he was 19 years old at the time. His age didn't matter to us. We christened him one Sunday and by the next Sunday he was officially my son. LaVelle could walk into a room and within ten minutes he would have everyone laughing to tears. He and Beulah were a lot alike in that way. They bonded tighter with each other than the others. LaVelle was a hard worker and very passionate about his walk with Christ. As much as he loved to sing, I think he liked directing choirs even more. He was a part of my family. I was happy, it had been so long since I felt like everything was going to be alright.

About a year and a half into our marriage, LaVelle and Beulah came into the house talking about how good a concert was that they had attended. After a few days of hearing them talk nonstop about their outing I asked, "What gospel concert and who took y'all?" They both looked at me and said, "J.W. and a lady friend."

"Oh really?" I replied, not wanting them to see how hurt I was. They looked at me, now curious about what happened. "You okay mama?" LaVelle asked several times. "I'll be fine, I've been through worse," I answered.

J.W. soon made his relationship public and asked for a divorce. His mother and my friend Ms. Hazel told me, "Hell naw, don't give him a divorce.

He's sitting on pensions and other benefits from working at Gerber Supply Company all those years." I looked at her and laughed.

"He wants to marry her, I guess."

"I don't give a damn what he wants. She can have him, but she can't have what is rightfully yours." Ms. Hazel spoke sternly. I kept looking at her shaking my head.

"Verna if you give J.W. that divorce, I'm going to beat your ass myself." I knew Ms. Hazel was serious from the look on her face.

When I decided to stay in my marriage after finding out about his affair, it was a very difficult choice. I was embarrassed and heartbroken. No one could understand how bad he'd hurt me. But in the end, I believe God blessed me for staying true to my vows. Without a divorce, I was still, legally, his wife when he passed away, and therefore received everything that was meant for me. No one could question it or fight it, because I was still his wife, and I had the papers to prove it.

Chapter 17

March 20, 1978, God blessed me with my first grandchild. Lolita gave birth to a beautiful little boy, Terry Ladette Hall. I knew the moment I held him, he was going to be spoiled for life. I hadn't realized my heart could grow anymore until his father put him in my arms. By June or July of that year things started to take a turn for the worse again. We had to move but had nowhere to go. I was forced to move my family, along with my grandson, Terry, into the Venus Motel. They had rooms that were charged at weekly rates. Lolita worked nights at Kettle Pancake House, she supplied the food for us while I worked to pay the weekly rate. It was a little cramped, but we had a roof over our heads. I thank God that He had blessed me with a car so she didn't have to catch the bus to the room late at night. It was a gift from one of my employees, therefore I had no notes and insurance wasn't mandatory back then. Each night I picked Lolita up from work, Terry rode in the car so he would go to sleep. I had him so spoiled, the nights his mother didn't work I still had to drive him around the block so he could go to sleep. Once we were back in our room he slept in my arms.

Randy moved to Dallas to live with Tit. I felt better knowing Randy was with her, because I knew she wouldn't let anyone hurt her. And, I also knew Tit would help raise my first granddaughter, Shandra Danyelle.

Life went on as we made our living arrangements work for us. One day after church Pastor and Sis. Booker called me into the office. Pastor explained that the church had purchased several homes to help members of the church and community have a place to live, until they were able to get back on their feet. They offered us the corner house for a low rental fee. It was the break I needed for me and my family. I don't know how Pastor and Sis. Booker found out we were renting that room at the motel and they never would tell me. They both agreed it wasn't a place that was safe for my family. They both gave me a hug and handed me the keys.

We lived on Jutland for a little over a year. While there Beulah gave birth to a beautiful little girl. Imagine my surprise when she told me her name, Verna. She named her daughter after me. I felt some kind of way, and that way had me feeling really good.

Still Standing

After Jutland we moved to Hogue Street.
Living on Hogue Street was good. After being there
for a while Tit and Bubba began to visit. When the
three of us got together our world felt complete.
Bubba would bring his girlfriend, Renee and their
daughter, Sherri Dawn. They would stay a couple of
weeks each visit. We would cook and stay up till the
wee hours of the morning, laughing, telling jokes, and
reflecting on how far God had brought us. Bubba
would sing for us like he did when we were little. He
sang gospel songs, but his favorite by far was Love
and Happiness by Al Green. He loved to sing all of his
music and we loved listening to him.

I turned 40 years old in 1981. We had a little
celebration. Al was a regular in the kitchen by now so
he helped me cook. We had a good time. I got to
spend time with my seven grandbabies, and thanked
God for the two that were on the way. I worked for
people who loved me and did what they could to help
make life easier for me. I belonged to a church where
I, my children and grandchildren were loved. We had
become part of the Greater Saint Matthew family and
it felt great. I drove the van for the youth and was
matron for the Young Adult Choir. I still sang in the
Senior Choir, and was now a part of a group Sis.
Booker had picked called The Chorale.

As driver of the van I delivered food to families
for the holidays. After finishing my deliveries one

evening I stopped at Kmart on Van Fleet to pick up a lay-a-way. As I was going to get into the van someone walked up behind me and put a knife to my throat. He asked me for all my money. I gave him all that I had. He got angry because he heard change rattling in my pocket and said I was holding back some money from him. He made me get in on the driver's side and slide onto the passenger's seat. I was forced to pull off all my clothes, except my shoes and socks. He assaulted me right there in the parking lot. He then drove off of the parking lot and headed to Kelso Elem. School where I was assaulted again. He had his knife pointed at my thigh, every time he hit a bump the knife would pierce my skin. I was so afraid. He then drove me to Adair Park and drove as far back in the park as he could go. He told me he was going to kill me when he got finished with me. I told him he didn't have to because I was going to die anyway because I didn't have my medicine. He was going to assault me again, but I pretended to have seizures. He opened the door and threw me out of the van.

With all the ice on the ground it was very cold and the fall bruised me up pretty bad. I got up and started walking back to the main road. I saw him parked on Cullen still sitting in the van. He didn't see me so I ran back into the park. I saw houses across the field. I had to climb a fence to get to the other side. I almost stepped on a cow as I jumped over the fence. I

Still Standing

don't know who was scared more, me or the cow. I ran across the field to one of the houses. No one answered so I turned to go to the next house when I saw some clothes hanging on the line. I got some of the clothes and a sheet and wrapped it around me. I stood there praying and scared. I knocked on the door of the next house. A lady opened the door and let me in. I told her what happened to me and she called the police. She was very kind and compassionate. She helped me to get warm and held my hand until the police arrived.

I was taken to Ben Taub hospital where I was checked out. I asked for a female nurse, but a male nurse entered the room. He had the nerve to ask me how did I allow someone to assault me like this, he acted as if it were my fault. I was so angry at him. At that point all I wanted was to go home. After all of the tests and questions, the police detective took me home. Needless to say my children were frantic with worry. It was after midnight and I was five hours late coming home. Once the detective told them what happened the boys were angry and my daughters cried a lot. Beulah sat by the side of the bed and watched over me. She called my employers. They cried more than my children did. I talked with Pastor and Sis. Booker, they encouraged me and prayed with me.

Some of my neighbors and a few men of the church went out looking for the guy who assaulted me, he was still driving the church van. The police found him out by the airport trying to rape a woman in one of the empty office buildings. I went downtown and picked him out of a picture book. I never had to see him again after that. I thank God for the strength of the men at Greater Saint Matthew. They were able to help me get through that ordeal more than the ladies. They were able to encourage me and let me know they would be more alert for the ladies of the church. The women wanted to help, but they either didn't know what to say or they would cry. I understood they loved me and couldn't bear the thought of me being hurt in such a way. Bro. Herb Wilkerson wrote a poem especially for me. It helped me understand, God saved me even though the enemy tried to take me out and destroy my joy again.

I wanted to start driving the van again right away, but Pastor Booker wouldn't hear of it. So, it was a few months before I was able to drive the van. My family was kinda upset, but it was what I had to do so I wouldn't be afraid to go out. God kept me here which meant I still had a job to do. After that incident, to this day, I must talk with someone in the family every day or they will come looking for me.

Chapter 18

Through the years we still moved a lot, but there was never a time we didn't have each other's back. I remember when we lived on Rickey Street. Times got a little tough, but by then we had learned to roll with the punches. The lights were turned off for a while and Albert did what he always did. Try to figure out a way to fix it, no matter how dangerous it seemed. I came in from work one Friday and the lights were on, well only on one side of the house. I asked how did that happen and everyone turned to look at Al. "Boy, what have you done?" I asked, scared of what his answer would be.

"Well, I kinda messed with the wires in the back, but could only get half of the house to work." I looked at him like one of us was going crazy and I knew it wasn't me.

"I paid the light bill and the lights will be on Monday. Now, please go undo what you have done."

"I will, Sunday, after church. We can't go through another weekend with no electricity." He smiled at me and I just shook my head. Before I could finish that conversation Entex had come and turned off the gas.

"What now? How am I supposed to cook?" I looked at my children and grandchildren and told them, "I'll figure something out, just let me lay down for a few minutes."

About an hour or so later I started smelling food. I didn't see anyone in the house so I looked out the window. Everyone was in the backyard, chilling. Lolita and Beulah had filled the small pool for the kids to play in, to keep cool. I went outside because I wanted to know where the smell of food was coming from. It was smelling really good and I was hungry. I stepped out the door, "What's going on? Y'all having a backyard party and I wasn't invited?" I laughed at them. I saw the picnic table all set and pointed at it. "Oh that, the food will be done in a minute," Al said. I looked around the yard and I saw no evidence of a grill, pit, or anything else that would produce the smell that was now making my stomach growl. "You looking for the food?" The girls asked laughing.

"I'm about to take the meat and beans off the pit now," Al said as he walked to the back of the yard. It was then I noticed smoke coming out of the ground.

Still Standing

Lolita, Beulah, and Don couldn't stop laughing at the look I had on my face. Al had dug a hole in the ground, lined it with foil paper, and took the racks out of my oven to use as the grill. He had wrapped a piece of metal in foil to use as the top of his in ground barbeque pit. "The corn and potatoes are on the table under that foil," he pointed at a pan sitting in front of me. "Well, let's eat and enjoy the pool party," Don laughed. We ate, got full, and put the rest on ice for the next day. True to his word, Al went to turn off the lights. I don't know what happened but we heard a loud noise and everything went black. "Al, where are you? Are you okay?" I kept shouting out to him. "I'll go get him," Don said. The door finally opened and both boys walked in. Don looked like he saw a ghost and Al looked like he'd stuck his finger in an electrical socket. "Boy, don't ever do that again! Do you hear me?" I fussed at him.

"I won't mama. I promise." As far as I know he hasn't and I thank God for that.

I thank God he didn't leave me without help in raising my children and helping with my grandchildren. LaVelle was always there and one of the best babysitters this side of heaven. He had structure and order down pat. The kids loved him and they knew when he was serious. He was a softie most of the time, but he was known to <u>try</u> to spank every now and then.

God also sent Robert Sims, to help get Don back on track. He wasn't a wild or disrespectful child, but he needed a strong male figure in his life to give him direction. Robert was what Don needed. I began to see the change in him right away, Al too. Robert kept them in church. They were both singing in The Young Adult Choir, but I knew they would need more than that to keep them out of trouble.

Robert started directing shows with Gospel Theater Company at church. Al, had found another niche besides cooking: working lights for the performances. The production company began to travel a lot and both boys, well young men were allowed to go. I knew they were in good hands with Robert. He didn't demand their respect, he had earned it the old fashioned way, with discipline, honesty, and loyalty. He also knew, he couldn't come back to Houston unless he had my two sons with him! I thank God he has always been there for Don, and later Shakira and he still is.

Along with LaVelle, God blessed me with more wonderful godchildren, Gloria Thompson, DeAndrea Bolden LaVergne, and Jared Alix. I believe my heart will never reach its full capacity of love I have for

Still Standing

children. My godchildren are an extension of my children. They give me a reason to keep fighting to go on. I've been blessed to see them graduate high school and college. I was blessed to be a part of DeAndrea's wedding. She was such a beautiful bride. Jared has always asked for only one thing, so I made sure each month he received a case of Ramen Noodles. They have opened their hearts to me and knowing I am a part of their lives is an awesome feeling.

Chapter 19

By the year 1990 all of my children were grown and gone. They girls were happily married and the boys were living on their own. I was 49 years old and finally living by myself. That was something I had never done before and it was very exciting. Even though everyone was gone, the one thing that never changed was my love for cooking and having my family around. Sunday dinner at my house had become the norm and something everyone looked forward too. It was at those dinners that I learned a lot about my children and how they felt about things they had seen or gone through. Even as they talked I knew there were things they weren't saying. I didn't know if they were trying to protect my feelings or they weren't ready to deal with whatever it was.

◊ ◊ ◊ ◊ ◊

With each Sunday dinner through the years I

Still Standing

noticed my children never lost their sense of humor or their quest for a better life. Not only was their love evident in how they lived, but in how they were raising their children. Between my children and grandchildren I have a funny bunch of people who are always already to eat and to make me laugh. I remember Bomb sitting at the dinner table and we could hear him saying, "Be still and get back in that bowl. I'm not playing." We all looked around.

"Bomb, who are you talking to?" Beulah asked.

"I'm talking to this dang crab that keeps trying to run away!"

"You mean the one in your gumbo?" Everyone asked.

"Yeah him. He knows I want to eat him so he keeps trying to get away." We all looked because we didn't know if he was serious or playing. It didn't matter because a few minutes later we watched as he ate that crab as if it was a part of his last meal. We laughed at him for a while. Poor crab, he lost! Then there was my grandson, Terry he was a huge Michael Jackson fan. I drove up into the driveway one evening and he came running out of the house with tears running down his face. I went into over protective grandma mode and was about to get somebody fast. "Grandma, grandma, I need your help really bad," he started to really cry now.

"What's wrong? Who did something to you?" He shook his head. "Grandma how much gas do you have in the van?" he asked between sobs. "Gas in the van? What's wrong? Where do you need to go?" He looked at me with those big brown sad eyes and said so seriously, "Michael Jackson's hair caught on fire. He got burned and I need to go see him. Do we have enough gas to go to California?" It was the grace of God that kept me from laughing on the spot. I got out of the van and gave him a hug. "Baby, grandma can't take you to California, but I can watch the news and let you know how he's doing. Will that be okay?" He hugged me as we walked into the house. "Grandma we gonna eat dinner while we wait for the news to come on?" I knew the food would win out at the end.

"Yep, come on so grandma can cook," I smiled at him. Grandma's job was done for the evening, comfort and cook is what I did best. Those are the memories that kept me going. Trust me there were many more, but those are for another time and another book.

As much as I love doing things and spending time with my children and grandchildren I wanted to find something I enjoyed, so I began to pray about it. I

Still Standing

didn't know what to ask God for because I didn't
know what I liked to do, besides be there for my
family. In 1995 God answered my prayer in a way I
never could have imagined. Greater Saint Matthew
went on its first church cruise. We rode the bus to the
cruise port. The closer we got to our destination the
more excited I became. I had never seen a cruise ship
before, so nothing could have prepared me for the awe
of seeing the Carnival Ecstasy Cruise Liner for the first
time. I looked at Beulah and she looked at me, then
we both started laughing. I think neither one of us
could explain what we were feeling so laughter was
the only way to express it. That was the beginning of
my love for the open seas and cruise ships. I have
been on twenty cruises since that first one and I pray
God blesses me to go on at least twenty more.

Chapter 20

In December of 2002 I sat on the sofa sorting through my Christmas decorations. I knew Don would be there in a few hours and he wanted to hang decorations up in the living room that night. After a couple hours passed, and everything was sorted out, Don still had not come home. I went to shower and get ready for bed. The door opened and Don came in. "Mama where are you?" He sounded too excited, knowing he was late.

"In my room. What's up?"

"I think I better show you." He walked in and put a newborn baby in my arms. He had a smile that spread across his entire face while I sat looking lost. "This is my daughter, Shakira." I was shocked.

"What? When did you get a baby?" I had a hundred questions, but the baby started to squirm. "She needs changing. Where is her stuff?" He gave

Still Standing

me a diaper bag with enough stuff for only a few hours. I cleaned her up, fed her, and laid her on the bed. Don stood there trying to supervise, but not knowing what to do. All I could do was laugh. "Boy, I got this." He smiled, "I know mama, I'm kinda nervous that's all." We stood there looking at the beautiful little girl that lay sleeping on my bed. The door opened and Al, Beulah, and Verna2 came in. "Mama, where are you?"

"Shhh, before you wake up the baby," Don said. They walked into the room. "Whose baby?" they asked in unisom.

"Mine." They all turned and looked at Don. You have to know my children to understand Al's next statement. "Boy, what nut done let you get her pregnant?" We all laughed.

"Don't you worry about all that," Don laughed at the look on his brother's face. They went back and forth with jokes while Beulah, Verna2, and I stood there looking at this precious baby laying in my bed still asleep. "Well son, the first thing you have to do in being a daddy, and bringing a baby home, is go to the store to get more milk and diapers."

"What? She has milk and diapers in her bag."

"She just drank one bottle and she'll be ready

for the other one as soon as she wakes up. And, six diapers won't last her through the night." He looked lost for a moment, but the laughter of his siblings and niece brought him back rather quickly. "Al, take your brother to the store and show him what to get." I laughed as Al led Don out the door teasing him again. Shakira stayed the weekend and went home. A few weeks later Shakira's mother called to ask if I would keep her for the Christmas Holidays. Of course I said yes. Beulah and Verna2 went to pick her up. That was the last we saw of her mother until it was time for me to go to court, to get custody of Shakira three years later.

Shakira is 13 years old now. I've never had to complain about being bored again after that December because she keeps me busy and laughing. I had forgotten what it was like to have a baby living in the house, but it was a change I wouldn't trade for anything in the world. I thank God that our family was very supportive in helping Don and I raise her. God blessed Shakira with two sets of wonderful godparents that help in nurturing and providing for her, Kim Ferguson and Shontell Ballard and her Uncle Al. Shakira is very good in school and knows obtaining a good education is very important. I try to keep her busy in other activities so she won't be distracted with things that are negative to her wellbeing. She'll probably be singing in the choir at church by the time

Still Standing

you're reading this. The great part about that is, she doesn't know yet that she'll be going to the next rehearsal. Because God has been so good to me, I'm able to do a lot for her that I wasn't able to do for my children when they were growing up. When I need help with uniforms and other things for dance or cheerleading, I thank God my grandson in law, Lee is always a call away and ready to help. One day Shakira will know and understand God brought her to our family on purpose, for her and for us.

Chapter 21

God has truly blessed me through the years. As great as life had become there were still some heartaches along the way. I had known God, the father, as a provider, a protector, and a shield. In 1998 I had to experience Him as a comforter, at the passing of my great grandson Malik Hall. He was a beautiful little boy. Seeing him smile was like a beacon from heaven. Seeing him fight against the odds of each surgery reminded me, *he's a part of me and he has the inner strength of his great-grandma*. Malik was three months old when God came for him. He wasn't with us long, but he left a lasting impact of love on our hearts.

In May of 2003 God called home my first godson, LaVelle. I stood at his bedside as he took his last breath. Oh my God that hurt. I remember them saying he was gone, I remember kissing him on the forehead and saying, "I love you son. I love you." I don't remember too much else about that night. I stood at his graveside as everyone began to walk off and thought, *Lord thank you for bringing LaVelle into my life, but I wish I had more time with him.* I stood there realizing no matter how much time you're given, it's never enough when it's someone you love that brings happiness into your life.

In October of 2008 I had to be a comforter and strength to my sister Tit as God called her daughter Gwen home to be with him. Tit, Bubba, and I, had a moment together. We just hugged and comforted each other. We learned years ago words weren't necessary for us, we just needed to touch each other and we knew everything would be okay.

In August of 2010 Beulah got an unexpected visit from Fort Bend's Sheriff's Dept. She called me, "Mama, the sheriff department just left saying we need to get to Scott and White Hospital in Temple, TX. Bomb has been admitted and they're saying he may pass before we get there." I heard her, but didn't hear her. I didn't know what to do or say, but I knew I couldn't panic. Verna2 (I know she prefer I not use her nickname,) rented a car and me and the girls got on the road. We didn't say much during the ride. Beulah stayed on top of things by staying in contact with the chaplain at the unit where he was housed. He put her in contact with Bomb's doctor and nursing staff so we could go right to ICU when we arrived.

We arrived at the hospital at 4:00pm and were met by his doctor outside of ICU. I didn't know what to expect when I walked into his room, but seeing my son hooked up to so many tubes and machines wasn't it. I could tell from the look on his sisters' faces they didn't expect for it to be that bad either. All four of us walked over to his bed slowly without saying anything. I touched his hands and they were already cold, it sent chills through my body. Watching and listening to the machines as they pumped air into his body was very overwhelming. The doctor came in and confirmed what we already knew, it was the machines working and not him breathing. He left out of the room so the girls and I could talk. We all agreed to have him taken off of the machines, but the ultimate decision was mine. That was the hardest piece of paper I've ever had to sign, in all my life. We stayed with him. We laughed and talked with him about how well he played the drums and how good he had kept his siblings in line. We teased about how Don and Al chickened out on coming at the last minute. I had begun to get tired, around 10:00pm Randy got us a room close by the hospital so I could lay down for a while and rest.

The phone rang at 11:10pm, it was Beulah telling us Bomb's vitals were dropping fast and we needed to come back to the hospital quickly. She and Lolita were standing by his bed when we walked in. Beulah was whispering in his ear again. I saw her doing that earlier. Randy moved on side of Lolita and rubbed his head, while Beulah stood next to me as I held his hand and spoke to him for the last time. "Bomb, mama is here. I love you son." A tear ran down his eye and at 11:42pm everything stopped. I laid my forehead on his and kissed him again. He looked so peaceful. The hospital staff gave us a few more minutes with him and the four ladies closest to him walked to the door, stopped and looked back one last time as he lay there in perfect rest.

On Friday June 12, 2015 I got a call from Baylor University Medical Hospital in Dallas, TX saying they found my brother unresponsive and he had been put on life support. My first thought was, *God no, not again.* I picked up Beulah, Saturday the 13th and we headed to Dallas. Thank God he prepared me for when I walked in his room. It was hard seeing my baby brother like that, tubes and machines were everywhere. The doctors wanted me to sign the release form to have him taken off of the life support machines. I couldn't do it. I told his grandchildren, "I don't know what you have to do to find your mother, but find her." They did and she came to the hospital. She signed the forms. Beulah and I stayed overnight and we left Sunday evening for home.

Once we got to Rosenberg, Beulah told me several times to let her run inside and get some clothes so she could drive me home. I assured her I was okay and I just wanted to be alone and get some rest. I stopped to get gas and got into a wreck trying to make a left turn. I believe that's when I started having a stroke.

For the next several days I stayed in bed all day. Beulah was gone to New Orleans, but she kept calling me. It seemed the more she called the more I was getting my dates, days, and times mixed up. She called Verna2 and told her what was going on. I remember my granddaughter Sheena coming by one day and another granddaughter Reecie coming by on another day. Beulah kept calling. She didn't like my behavior so she called our close friend, Donna Bolden, who is a nurse. Beulah called Verna2 and told her all Donna had said for her to do.

On Thursday June 18th Verna2 came by to take me to Methodist Hospital in Sugar Land. I was admitted for testing and the doctors told her I had had a stroke. It didn't affect me physically, but it started stripping away a lot of my memory. Verna2 stayed at the hospital with me, watching over me and talking with my doctors. We got a call, the evening of June 19th that Bubba had passed away. I knew it was just a matter of time, even in knowing that, a part of my heart seemed to have left me. My brother, the only brother I had left, was gone.

By Sunday the doctors discharged me so I could

Still Standing

go home. Verna2 picked me up from the hospital and we went to my granddaughter, Stephanie's house. I think they were celebrating Lolita's birthday. I sat in the midst of people whom I knew was my family. Their faces were familiar, but I had no clue of who was who. I knew who my children were, and I recognized Terry and Reecie when they came through the door. I smiled a lot, but I didn't say much. Gloria Alix and her mom, Mama Davis came by. I hugged them and I knew I should have known them because of the love and concern they had for me. I asked Beulah and Verna2 who they were on our way home. They were shocked for a moment knowing I didn't recognize who everyone was, including my great grandchildren. I just knew in my heart everyone loved me and was glad to see me out of the hospital.

Beulah brought her clothes from Rosenberg to stay with me. I started getting lost in my own house. I stood in the front hallway one day just looking around. "Mama, what are you doing?" Beulah asked.

"I'm looking for my bedroom." Beulah came over and took me by the arm and led me to my room. I sat on the bed looking confused. I remember asking for dinner because I thought it was eight in the evening, but it was ten in the morning. Then I asked, "Are we going to church today?"

"No mama, today is Monday. You missed

church yesterday. You were in the hospital and then we went to Stephanie's" she answered softly. I nodded my head and went back to my bedroom.

I remember eating breakfast and getting ready for work. "I can drive. I'm ok." I said as we walked out the door. I got my keys and got behind the wheel of the car. I pulled out of the drive way and headed in the opposite direction of where I worked. Beulah called Al and he gave her directions to my job. Once I got about two blocks from the house my memory started coming back. "I know where I am now." By the time I pulled into the driveway and got out of the car, my employer, Darwin walked up. "Verna, how are you and what are you doing here?" he asked, concern all over his face. Beulah got out and talked with him for a minute. He turned and looked at me. "Verna let Beulah take you back home and you rest. You probably shouldn't drive until you see your doctor tomorrow," he told me and Beulah. Darwin and I took a picture together and Beulah drove me home.

I remember being at the doctor's office with Beulah. I sat there and listened in shock as Dr. Greer told Beulah I couldn't drive for a month. I started to protest until she picked up her phone to call Verna2. The doctor looked at the both of us because I kept saying, "No, you don't have to call her. I'll give you the keys."

Still Standing

"Who is that?" he asked. He was worried until we both started laughing. "That's my granddaughter and she's not gonna let me drive at all." I looked between the both of them. "Can I drive to the store?" I asked hoping to get a little break. He dropped the bomb real quickly. "No! You are not to drive at all." Dr. Greer turned to Beulah. "You and the family need to ask your mama lots of questions. The ones that will make her think. She needs to get her brain active. The deeper she has to think about her answers the quicker she will regain her memory." Beulah asked and answered a lot of questions. I guess when she had all of the answers she needed we left for home.

Beulah stayed at the house taking care of me and making sure I took all my medicines and on time. She wouldn't let me cook because I kept for getting what I was cooking or how long I had been cooking it. I was still getting lost in my own home. I couldn't remember events and people. Every now and then after we'd sit at the table and talk she would have an unexplained look on her face. Well, one night I found out what the look was about. Beulah thought I was asleep, but I could hear her crying. She was talking to her husband, Thomas. "It's so hard seeing her like this. She has always been the strength of our family and the one who takes care of us." She listened.

"I know, I'm strong when she's awake. I don't know how to help her and that's the most frustrating."

I listened as Beulah continued.

"That's my mama. I'm doing everything the doctors told me to do. She's getting better, but it's still hard." She talked for a few more minutes and hung up the phone. She came in to check on me and I laid there like I was sleeping. We got up the next day and I knew I was going to get better, not just for me, but for my children and grandchildren. And, I needed to be able to drive again and Beulah wasn't hearing that as long as my memory was like it was, barely there.

Bubba's family in Dallas started planning for his service. They needed answers that only I could give and I think that helped a lot, it made me think about dates and events from our past. I talked to Tit a few times to make sure she was okay. She was getting weak and I know losing Bubba wasn't good because they were so close. I was getting a lot of my memory back. It felt good to know who people were again. I still got twisted around in my directions so I knew driving was still out of the question. I remember sitting at the table talking with Beulah before she went home. "I don't know how long Tit is going to make it without Bubba. I hope she makes it to her birthday and Thanksgiving. I would like one more holiday with my sister."

"I know mama. I hope she makes it too." Beulah gave me a hug and finished packing her stuff.

Still Standing

Her oldest son DeAnthany would be here soon to take her home.

Of course when Beulah went back to Rosenberg Verna2 took my keys and put them way out of my reach. Shakira was home and helping me around the house. Thank God she had been watching me cook because now all of her cooking skills were about to be tested, (she did really well.) Reecie, Verna2, and my great grandson Brian took turns taking me where I needed to go. I didn't have to worry about going to work because my grandsons Terry, Steven, DeAnthany, and my grandson in law Lee made sure I had money to buy food and pay my bills. I talked with a child, grandchild, or great grandchild on the phone every day. Al bought food over, and Lillian cooked and sent food over by Beulah. I was getting better each day and I liked it.

We held Bubba's home going service July 2, 2015 in Dallas, TX. Tit and I got to say goodbye to Bubba at the funeral home on our way to the church. The memorial service was nice. Bubba was cremated later that day. We got back to Houston that evening. Later that night Sharon had to admit Tit into Memorial Herman NW Hospital. I kept busy at the house trying not to worry. Tit and I had already talked about two weeks before Bubba passed. She was tired and ready to go home to be with the Father. She was alert, but getting weaker by the day, I could hear it in her voice.

I had to go see her, touch her, and hear her voice. Verna2 took me to the hospital. I sat there holding her hand. She didn't talk much and when she did it was barley a whisper. Once again we knew many words were not needed. When I got ready to leave I kissed her on the forehead and told her I love her. She looked me in the eyes and I knew she was ready to go be with her twin. A few days later Sharon called and told me Tit had been moved to Kindred NW/Transitional Care and Specialty Hospital. July 31st Sharon called to tell me my sister had just passed away. I thanked her for calling me and sat there for a moment. The only thing that seemed to register was, *my sister and brother were gone. They're together, yet still gone.*

Once the word had gotten around to the family my children and grandchildren did what I knew they would do, gather around me to keep me busy and strong. Sharon kept me involved in the planning stages and that helped me most of all. Tit's funeral was Friday August 7, 2015. Sitting on that front row I knew it would be the last time I would see my sister on this side. We had been through so much and God brought us through it together. Sharon asked me to speak at the service. Once again God gave me more strength than I knew I had. I sat at Clara/Tit's graveside as the final words were spoken over her by the funeral director. I didn't hear much of what he said. I was silently pondering in my heart that my

Still Standing

sister and brother were together again, but this time in perfect peace. I didn't feel sad, I knew God left me here because He has more for me to do. I guess writing this book is just a part of it.

Chapter 22

There's a cool breezing blowing today so I decided to sit outside and write. I don't have to look far to see how much God has blessed me. My children are doing well and I am so proud of them. Lolita and her husband Curtis are entrepreneurs, they are founder and owners of Caws Cracklins. They have 33 flavors and they taste great. Lolita can still out braid anyone I know. She has practiced on our heads for a whole lot of years and it shows in the greatness of her work. She now has her own line of hair products named Heavenly Hair.

Myranda is engaged to Donald Williams. She has her own daycare, Children Are Us. She has her own style of teaching and every child that has gone through her daycare over the last 20 years still love and respect her. She owns and operates a yard and landscaping service. Her yard work is great and she has also been known to hang sheetrock, put in floors, and paint a room or two. She's a hard worker and takes pride in all that she does. Right now she's taking a break to spoil her first grandson Emanuel.

Beulah is married to Thomas Jr. She is the founder and CEO of her publishing company, BeNeveu Words, Inc. She's an author, poet, and speaker. She has self published three books, Bracie, A Cry For Home, and Botched But Beautiful. She is currently in the process of working on her first publishing project, my book, Still Standing. She's also studying to become a certified Christian Chaplain.

Don has always been a hard worker. He loves to sing and play the congos. Don is not in good health, but like his mother he is a fighter.

The love of cooking has never left Albert. He is owner of Al's Spice One, where he caters awesome lunches all around Houston and the surrounding areas. In his spare time he works as a carpenter, building kitchen cabinets.

My grandchildren are just as awesome. I have college graduates, teachers, entrepreneurs, models, engineers, and barbers. All of them are hard workers. The fourth generation is just beginning to move on to higher education. Brian and Christopher have graduated High School and are proud Texas Southern University Tigers.

I know how proud I am of them, but I wanted them to share their thoughts on how life has been with me as their mother, grandmother, and great grandmother.

Lolita: Mama, I am so proud of you. You have always been my support and my reason for being the person I am today. Mom, you are a strong and inspiring woman. I've seen you go through some things most women couldn't handle or make it through. You always have a smile on your face even when you are hurting on the inside. You will always be my Shero. The fact that you're still standing, after some of the things you went through, lets me know I can never give up. Thank you mama for always being there for me, even when you couldn't be there physically you were there spiritually. I love you with all of me!!!

Myranda: Mama, I have always known that you were a very strong and loving woman. I know some people say that hardships made them hard or bitter, but it doesn't have to be like that. It all depends on how they want to overcome and live their lives. Mama, with God in your life you were able to overcome the obstacles and still have love in your heart, and not just for your children, but for everyone. Although this book doesn't speak on everything that you had to endure it's enough to make one cringe. I wouldn't say I would ever go back to those days. No,

Still Standing

I take that back. I would like to go back so I can whip his a** Anyway, mom you speak for all women who have gone through or are going through something similar, that they can stand strong and overcome it. The love that I have for you can't really be summed up on paper, nor can anything contain or hold the amount of love, respect, and admiration I have for you. I will always be thankful because you have instilled great qualities in me.

Beulah: Mama, you have always been my example of a godly mother even when I didn't understand you were always about doing the Father's business. Knowing what and how much you've had to endure and overcome so your children could live a life of peace has humbled me beyond words. As I sit here and type all I can do is cry. The only words I can say now are, "Thank You!" Thank you for every sacrifice you've ever given for me. Thank you for always listening and not judging. Thank you for always loving me, but most of all, thank you for always praying for me. May God give you all of your heart's desire and may He bless your latter to be greater than your beginning. I love you!

Donald: Mama you are the sweetest and strongest woman I know. I respect and honor you more than you'll ever know. I guess, that's because I just don't say it enough. You made sure we were always taken care of. You made sure we were always fed, even when it meant you didn't eat. I remember walking to Dan Ingles store waiting for you to get off the bus so I could pack the bags home. I can't ever remember hearing you complain about being tired. You just did what you'd always done, survive for you and for us. I still think about how you opened our home to other kids and you treated them so nice I would be jealous. I know now you were always doing what God had called you to do. Mama, do you remember during one of my whippings I fell on the floor pretending to have a seizure? You kept whipping my butt, so I finally came to my senses and got up from the floor and cried harder so you could stop. It worked! No matter how tough it got you never let us stop laughing. Mama, you are my queen. You are the queen of love, kindness, and forgiveness.

Albert: First, I would like to thank God for blessing me with you for my mama. There were a lot of things I didn't understand while growing up, but I've come to know how strong and powerful you are. I understand now, how you've always trusted God without saying a word. There were times when it seemed like it wasn't enough food for us, yet you still opened your doors to feed someone else. You always helped people with a place to live, even when they wouldn't do anything to contribute to the household. No matter what obstacles came along, and there were many, you always showed us, God has a way of

125

working things out. Mama, thank you for keeping us in church because you knew that would always be the foundation we'd need to make it through life. In closing I'm proud to say, "Mama, you are great in every sense of the word." I wouldn't change anything about how we were raised as long as I got to keep you as my mom. Mama, I love you and I appreciate you.

Shakira: Mama, you are the strongest woman I know. You had already raised your six children when I came into the picture. You took me in and showered me with love. When it was time to go to court, without hesitation you fought to keep me and raise me as your own. I know it wasn't easy for you to start over with an infant, but you have been the best mother ever to me. You have molded me and have taught me so much about life. You have always been there for me and made sure I had everything I need. Well, here it is 14 years later and you're still standing strong as the greatest mother ever! From the bottom of my heart I thank you and I love you.

Terry; thoughts from the grandchildren: When you think of grandma, you think foundation. My grandma, ok, our grandma is the foundation of this family. Grammy you hold us up when we get weak. You're the shoulder we cry and lean on. When things around us are not going well and falling apart, you are the glue that keeps us together. Not many grandmothers will go out of their way for all of their grandkids, but you do it without a fuss. Grammy, you are like no other. You're the one who never judges, but speaks wisdom so that we can sit up straight and think about our decisions. Grammy you're an original that can't be duplicated, your smile lights up every room you enter. When you have a woman of God on your team, there's no way you're going to lose. Grammy you are our coach and we love you very much. We all chose a word or phrase to describe your character:

DeAnthany: Resilient, Terry: Amazing, DeJuan: Caring, Sheena: Strong

Sharon: Loving, Rachel: Genuine, Shandra: Giving

Sherelle: Sincere, Stephanie: Virtuous, Albert II: Surperb,

Steven: Accepting, Courtney: Dependable, Dominique: Forgiving,

Verna2: My inspiration, Reecie: The One (One of a kind)

DeRaymond: Sugar to our sweet tea

Still Standing

Brian; thoughts from the great grandchildren: Dear Great Grandmother, we love you so much. Our generation began in the latter part of the 1990's. We are the ones everyone says are super spoiled. Well, I'm admitting it, you have us spoiled, but so is the generation before us, lol. Grammy, you have been there for us all, LITERALLY! You've always been a call away. You've never turned away from your family and we thank you and appreciate you for that. You love us all equally and generously. I'm all grown up now, and I speak not only for me, but for all 52 of your great grandchildren, you haven't changed a bit. You're the God fearing, loving, and most beautiful great grandmother this side of heaven.

We pray God keeps blessing you and that He'll let you see another generation be born so you can spoil them too.

Epilogue

It's 2016 and I sit here with a heart of gratitude. I don't have time to complain about what has been or what should have been. I praise God the Father for bringing me through every trap Satan had set for me. I realize if I hadn't gone through such a tough beginning I wouldn't be as strong as I am now. I thank God for Joshua 1:9 that says, *Be strong, and of a good courage; be not afraid, neither be thou dismayed: for the LORD thy God is with thee whitersoever thou goest.* I knew through it all God was with me. Through every difficult time the LORD was shaping me into the woman of God I am today. I didn't understand then, like I do now the spiritual legacy I was building for my children, my family. I can see now my legacy's foundation is built on an eternal faith in God through Jesus Christ. I now understand John 10:28, from the moment of my conception God had placed me in His hand and nothing or no one can ever pluck me out. As I watch my children I know God

Still Standing

loves me and He had a greater plan all along. So many nights I had to cry, but as I see the joy that has come from the tears that were counted by God himself I know everything really is going to be alright.

As I read the thoughts of my children, grandchildren, and great grandchildren I want them to know how humbled I am. I want them to know I fought because of them! I fought for them! I'm going to keep watching, fighting, and praying for them. I know if it were not for them I don't know how I would have had the strength to go on. Knowing that they could see God living in me made me press my way through. I pray as they face the daily challenges of life they have learned that God can, and will, bring them through anything as long as they live within His will. I pray that above all else they all know I love them with a love that can only come from God the Father because it is true, it is loyal, and it is eternal.

Today I pray that each woman that reads this book is inspired to trust in the courage that God has put inside of you. No matter how difficult a situation may seem God is greater than what you face. And though I contemplated and tried to commit suicide it is never God's plan for us. His peace can and will sustain you. Don't be afraid to get the help that wasn't so freely given when I was young. Remember, God created you beautiful. You are His. He has no respect of person, what God has brought me through, He can do the same for you. It is the Father's desire that you stand in the power of His might. One day you, like I, can praise the Lord with your hands lifted high thanking Him that you too are victorious. My steps have become slower and someday they will become few, but today I rejoice because God has saw fit to have me, Still Standing!

About the Author

Verna Davis LaCour is a native of DeQuincy, LA. She was raised and attended school in Angleton, TX. She is the mother of six children, grandmother of 17 and great grandmother of 52. She is the godmother of three and has a great love for all children.

Verna is an active member of Greater Saint Matthew Church. She attends Wednesday night Bible Study and Monday night Bible Study for women. She sang in the Senior Choir where she did lead vocals on one of the church's first album recordings. Verna also sang with the Women's Choir, Celestial Voices Choir, and the Greater Saint Matthew Chorale, a small group chosen and directed by the late Dr. Theola Booker.

Verna loves to cruise the open seas. She enjoys cooking, sewing, playing volleyball, and listening to gospel music.

Made in the USA
Columbia, SC
17 June 2024

36732766R00074